DATE DUE

9-7			
10-10 >			
3/14			
GAYLORD			PRINTED IN U.S.A.

ALSO BY HAL URBAN

LIFE'S GREATEST LESSONS:
20 Things That Matter

POSITIVE WORDS, POWERFUL RESULTS:
Simple Ways to Honor, Affirm, and Celebrate Life

HAL URBAN

CHOICES THAT CHANGE LIVES

15 WAYS TO FIND MORE PURPOSE, MEANING, AND JOY

A Fireside Book
Published by Simon & Schuster
New York   London   Toronto   Sydney

FIRESIDE
Rockefeller Center
1230 Avenue of the Americas
New York, NY 10020

FIRESIDE and colophon are registered trademarks
of Simon & Schuster, Inc.

For information regarding special discounts for bulk purchases,
please contact Simon & Schuster Special Sales at 1-800-456-6798
or business@simonandschuster.com

Designed by William Ruoto

Manufactured in the United States of America

10 9 8 7 6 5 4 3 2 1

Library of Congress Data Control Number: 2005054666

ISBN-13: 978-0-7432-5770-1
ISBN-10:   0-7432-5770-7

This book is dedicated to

CATHY URBAN

My most trusted adviser, greatest source of encouragement, and best friend.

We must make the choices that enable us to fulfill the deepest capacities of our real selves.
—Thomas Merton

Purpose, Meaning, and Joy

Purpose is the place where your deep gladness meets the world's needs.

—FREDERICK BUECHNER

Meaning is strength. Our survival may depend on our seeking and finding it.

—VIKTOR FRANKL

This is the true joy in life, the being used for a purpose recognized by yourself as a mighty one.

—GEORGE BERNARD SHAW

Contents

Preface

Goals, Flaws, Quotes, and Self-Help Books

Some random thoughts from the author

TWO MAIN GOALS: TO BE "UPBEAT" AND "INSPIRING"

Thousands of people whom I've never met have more influence on my writing than they could possibly imagine. These are the people who read my books and graciously take the time to tell me how their lives have been enriched. Few things in life are more powerful than positive feedback. It affects us in two ways: First, it affirms us—it tells us that we did something well, that our hard work was worth the effort, and that it was appreciated. Second, it encourages us to continue—to build on what we've achieved and to add to it. These are exactly the effects the phone calls, letters, and e-mails from people of all ages and walks of life have had on this writer.

Two of the words that have been used most frequently by these readers are *upbeat* and *inspiring*. Since these happen to be two of my favorite words, as well as two of my main goals in writing, they're always music to my ears. Another positive word that's come up often is *hope,* as in, "You've given me hope." These usually come from readers experiencing hard times: prisoners, people going through a divorce or other form of loss, and those coping with illness, addiction, or financial problems. While I make no effort or claim to be a therapist, it's deeply gratifying to learn that my writings have helped other people. I pray that this book will also be upbeat and inspiring and offer hope.

CONFESSIONS OF A FLAWED AUTHOR

> *The common perception that good people have fewer flaws is*
> *wrong. It is not a matter of more or fewer flaws. It is the*
> *willingness to change them that counts.*
>
> —LOUIS A. TARTAGLIA, M.D.

A few years ago I was being interviewed on a Columbus, Ohio, TV station about my first book, *Life's Greatest Lessons.* The interviewer said, "So, we finally get to meet someone who has it all figured out. I guess you're just up and happy all the time. Tell us how you do it." I laughed—not at the interviewer, but at myself. I told him the same thing I tell all the people who contact me: Like everyone else, I'm a work in progress. I have some major flaws that I've been working on for a long time, and I don't claim to have it all figured out. But I'm a lot closer now that I was ten or twenty years ago, mainly because of the mistakes I've made and what I've learned from them. And I'm not "up and happy all the time." I don't think anyone is. Fortunately, I am most of the time simply because of two of the greatest truths I've learned along the way:

1. Every mistake is an opportunity to improve and grow.
2. It's never too late to change.

You've probably noticed that in the back of almost every book, including this one, there's a page "about the author." We usually learn about the writer's education, career achievements, awards and honors, other books, and current pursuits. Everything is positive and impressive. But because of the nature of this book, I think it's equally important to reveal up front some of the author's weaknesses and struggles. The pain from them has helped me make better choices, find more peace of mind and joy, and lay the groundwork for writing this book.

The first five chapters are about humility, patience, empathy, forgiveness, and giving. These are qualities in which I was sorely lacking for many years. They reveal the worst of my weaknesses and most difficult struggles. I write about these great virtues now, not because I claim to have them, but because I'm working on them, and because I seek the inner peace and joy that flow from them. On many occasions in the past I damaged my own life and hurt others because of pride, impatience, insensitivity, resentment, or just plain old selfishness. These were my personal demons for many years. In the last few decades I've made some progress in dealing with them, but still have a way to go. The process, though, has been incredibly rewarding, and I hope worth sharing with others.

Someone who knows me from previous years is likely to pick up this book, see that the first chapter is about humility, and say, "He's the *last* person who should be writing about humility." While I would fully understand such a comment, I would disagree for one simple reason: Sometimes those of us who have made the biggest mistakes are the ones most qualified to share what we've learned from them. A case in point: I have a dear friend who almost ruined his life several years ago due to excessive drinking. He lost his wife, his home, his job, and most of his money. After hitting bottom, he finally admitted that he had a problem and started attending AA meetings. He slowly rebuilt his life. He stopped drinking, worked hard, saved money, remarried, and bought a new home. He retired a few years ago from a prestigious job in finance. No one is more qualified than he is to talk to others about the damage that can result from too much alcohol. And that's exactly what he's been doing for more than twenty years. He's helped countless people correct the course of their lives. I hope I can do the same thing, but in a different way. I've never had a drinking problem, but I've had numerous battles with personality defects that have resulted in great pain, including the loss of friendship. Maybe my weaknesses and the attempts to correct them will help other people who struggle in similar ways. There are few things more joyous than overcoming weaknesses, no matter what kind they are. Celebrating triumphs of the human spirit, especially when it involves personal growth, is one of the great rewards of life.

Since 1995 I've been speaking to teachers and students at all grade levels. I also talk to parents, people in business and government, and members of churches. These talks, no matter what the topic, always include some of my biggest mistakes and the lessons I've learned from them. I tell every audience, "I don't have all the answers, and I'm not telling you that you should do everything I do. I just want to share with you some things that seem consistently to work most of the time. Try them out, tweak them to fit your needs, and discard the ones that don't work for you."

I'm saying the same thing here to my readers. I don't want to tell anyone else how to live his or her life. I just hope some of my own struggles and the discoveries that resulted from them will deepen your understanding about how life works and what's essential for a life with purpose, meaning, and joy. And I hope they'll be things that work for you, too.

ABOUT MY COAUTHORS AND THEIR QUOTES

I love quotes because it is a joy to find thoughts one might have,
beautifully expressed with much authority by someone
recognized as wiser than myself.

—MARLENE DIETRICH

This isn't a book that comes from my great storehouse of wisdom—mainly because I don't have one. It's a book that comes from a great storehouse of wisdom that's been passed down to us for thousands of years. Countless wise people have graced the earth both before us and in the present, and have left great treasures of advice on how to lead good and meaningful lives. These brilliant people, some famous and some not so famous, some long dead and some still living, are my coauthors.

In my first two books I used hundreds of quotes from other writers. Many readers expressed appreciation for them and have shared with me the many ways in which they've been put to use. Most people, even those who aren't fond of reading, seem to enjoy and value a good quote. We marvel at some wise person's ability to make a statement of great meaning and impact while using only a few words. The beauty of these quotes is that they crystallize important ideas for us. They're short, get right to the point, are full of common sense and wisdom, and are easy to remember. We treasure the insight expressed in these simple maxims.

There are single thoughts that contain the essence of a whole
volume, single sentences that have the beauties of a larger work.

—JOSEPH JOUBERT

I have again relied heavily on quotes from other authors. In fact, this book is built largely around the great wisdom that's been handed down to us for generations. I firmly believe that all the important observations and statements regarding human behavior were made long before I came along. So there isn't anything here that hasn't been said before. But the observations are, I hope, organized and presented in a way that's relevant and helpful. It's always been my aim to shed new light on old truths and then apply them to life in the present. I hope you'll find here some important reminders about what it takes to make the right choices, be a person of good character, find more purpose and meaning, and increase in wisdom and joy.

My only regret about the quotes is that they're not more gender sensitive. Many of them are old, and people long ago wrote about "man" instead of the human race. I couldn't change them from how they were originally written, but do hope you'll read them as insights and suggestions regarding all human behavior.

ABOUT "SELF-HELP" BOOKS

When *Life's Greatest Lessons* was self-published several years ago, someone told me that I needed to have a category for the book, and to write it in the upper lefthand corner of the back cover. I came up with "Personal Growth/Inspiration." This seemed the most logical, since I originally wrote the book for young people whom I wanted to help grow personally. I also wanted to inspire them to become the best persons they could be. This category worked fine until I sold the book to Simon & Schuster. They sell a lot of books to bookstores, but none of those stores seem to have a section called "Personal Growth/Inspiration." So my books end up in a section called "Self-Help."

This is one of the great oxymorons of all time, and a term that I've never liked, mainly because it contradicts itself. If people are going to help themselves, why would they want to read a book written by someone else? Doesn't that defeat the purpose of helping yourself? You'd think that the people who run bookstores and appreciate written words so much could come up with a more fitting category for books like these. Please understand that I'm not knocking all the books you find in the "self-help" section of a bookstore. Many of them are wonderful. Some of the best books I've ever read were found in that section, and they've greatly enriched my life. They inspired me and helped me grow personally, but they didn't really "self-help" me.

Regardless of where you found *this* book, I hope it enlightens and inspires you to become a more complete person no matter what mistakes you've made, and no matter what stage of life you're currently in. One of the great joys of life is knowing that there's always room for increased self-awareness and personal growth. We can be better, happier, and wiser at any time we choose. I hope this book helps you in that joyful pursuit.

It's never too late to be what you might have been.

—GEORGE ELIOT

Introduction

FIVE REASONS FOR WRITING THIS BOOK

1. TO EXPLAIN MORE FULLY THE IMPORTANCE OF CHOICE

"We live by choice, not by chance" is the title of chapter four in *Life's Greatest Lessons*. We considered using it as the title of this book because of the impact this simple truth had on so many readers. I recall vividly that while I was on a media tour for the book in January 2003, virtually every TV and radio host wanted to talk about the "choices chapter" first. You would have thought that I'd made some startling discovery that was going to dramatically change millions of lives. But the truth is that choices have been around for as long as humans have. It's truly amazing how many people are either unaware, or forget, that they're making choices almost all of the time—little ones that are unimportant, and big ones that can change our lives for good or for bad. This book is about some of those big choices.

I explained in my first book that I was educated by the Jesuits at the University of San Francisco. If you're unfamiliar with the Jesuits, they can probably best be described as a teaching order of Catholic priests, founded by St. Ignatius Loyola, who place great emphasis on philosophy, logic, ethics, and the free will. This is where I first learned the importance of living by choice. Rather than create us as mere puppets without a mind of our own, God gave us our greatest gift—the free will, or the power to choose. It's one of those great lessons that you never forget.

That great lesson was reinforced several years later when I discovered a marvelous little book that's now considered by many to be a classic. It's called *Your Greatest Power,* and was written in 1953 by J. Martin Kohe. The book opens with this sentence:

**YOU ARE THE POSSESSOR OF A GREAT AND
WONDERFUL POWER.**

A little further down the first page, Kohe points out that most people live in total unawareness of it:

> *Millions of people are complaining about their lot, disgusted with life . . . and the way things are going, not realizing that there is a power which they possess which will permit them to take a new lease on life. Once you recognize this power and begin to use it, you can change your entire life and make it the way you would like to have it . . . filled with joy.*

Kohe points out that the most amazing thing about this power is that it's accessible to everyone, regardless of age or position in life. It doesn't require intelligence, education, achievement, or special talents. It's given to all of us at birth. All we need to do is recognize it. What is this great power? Kohe answers this question on page nine:

**THE GREATEST POWER
THAT A PERSON POSSESSES IS
THE POWER TO CHOOSE.**

Whether you refer to it as "free will" as the Jesuits do, or "your greatest power" as Kohe does, it's a fact of life: We really do live by choice, not by chance. In that first book I listed nine principal choices we make: our character, our values, how we treat others, how we handle adversity, how much we'll learn, what we'll accomplish, our belief system, our purpose, and our attitude. While these are important, there are many other choices we make daily that also help determine the quality of our lives. I want to share fifteen of those choices with you in this book.

There are alternatives. Options. We cannot choose not to choose.
—LEWIS B. SMEDES

2. TO COMPLETE SOME UNFINISHED BUSINESS

In the introduction to *Life's Greatest Lessons: 20 Things That Matter,* I asked the question, "Why 20?" There was no profound reason, and I never claimed that they were the *only* great lessons life teaches us. They were simply some of the most basic truths about how life works that I wanted to pass on to my sons and to my students. What had begun as a letter to them eventually became a book for kids, then a book for people of all ages. Apparently, a lot of adults appreciated being reminded about the importance of good character and what I called "old-fashioned goodness."

When I wrote the original table of contents it had thirty life lessons, and I knew there were actually many more than that. But the book would have been too long, so I pared it down to the essentials. Some of those essentials are a good attitude, respect, hard work, self-discipline, kindness, honesty, laughter, and thankfulness. Now thirteen years have passed, and those ten great lessons that I left out remain as unfinished business. In addition, I've learned a few more (some very painfully) that I'd also like to pass along. The lessons in this book are a little different. They're not as basic or obvious as the original twenty. They might be described as the ones we learn as we progress through the higher grades in the school of life. Some of these new lessons are also more challenging. We learn about virtues like humility, patience, forgiveness, empathy, and giving at a greater cost—the sacrifice of self. But when mastered, these and the other lessons included here bring even greater joy and deeper meaning to our lives.

3. TO THANK AND HONOR MY READERS

There are no words in any language that could adequately express the depth of my appreciation for the hundreds of people who've written, called, and e-mailed me after reading both *Life's Greatest Lessons* and *Positive Words, Powerful Results*. They've thanked me, shared their own insights and valuable lessons, made suggestions, sent me quotes and poems, pointed out useful books and websites, made me both laugh and cry, and have affirmed and encouraged me. It's because of this encouragement that I went from being a self-published author to a Simon & Schuster author with a much wider audience. These wonderful people have also urged me to continue to "preach the gospel" of good character and to continue writing. These additional life lessons are for them.

4. TO SATISFY THE NEEDS OF A TEACHER

I spent thirty-five wonderful years being a teacher both in a high school and in a university. Though I left the classroom, I never wanted to stop teaching or, for that matter, learning. Fortunately, I'm now a traveling teacher, and my students include other teachers, kids of all ages, parents, business people, and members of churches. I still get to teach, but I don't have to correct papers, turn in grades, or attend faculty meetings.

The biggest change, though, is that I'm no longer required to do what teachers spend most of their time doing—preparing lesson plans. But old habits are hard to break. I continue to write new lessons simply because there's so much to be learned and to be passed on. It's what a teacher does. For several years I've been writing these lessons in a journal and other notebooks in the hope of eventually sharing them with others. Many teachers (from elementary school through college) who've been using my first book have asked me if there would be more great lessons. Now there are.

Rabbi Harold Kushner, in his brilliant book *When All You Ever Wanted Isn't Enough*, says that we are all teachers:

> *We all teach, officially and unofficially, not only the classroom teacher or college professor addressing a group of students, but the experienced bookkeeper or factory worker passing tips on to the new arrival, because having an impact on another person, shaping his or her life in some small but vital way, is one of the most enduring satisfactions we will know. We teach because we need to share.*

Please join me and my fellow teachers in our efforts to make a positive impact while passing on more of the great lessons of life.

5. TO EXPLORE THE SOURCES OF WISDOM

The first title I thought of for this book was "Wisdom Is Earned." It was to be about more life lessons that lead to life's ultimate prize. But my publisher and editor weren't as keen on it as I was, for a variety of reasons. Because they know much more than I do about what works and what doesn't in the book industry, I listen to them. We changed the key word in the title from "wisdom" to "choices," and gave the book a more upbeat tone. The next-to-last chapter here is about wisdom, and I'm convinced that if we make the right choices we can attain it.

For many years I thought wisdom was the result of a natural process: We get older, we get wiser. While there's an element of truth to this common belief, it's far from the entire story. Not all elderly people are wise, and some young people are wise beyond their years. Real wisdom is understanding how life works and living it well, regardless of age.

I wrote *Life's Greatest Lessons* the year I turned fifty. A lot of nice people read it, wrote to me, and told me I was wise. But I didn't feel wise. I thought the book was based mostly on common sense. Although related, there's a big difference between common sense and wisdom. There's also a difference between success (the topic of that first book) and making choices that help us increase in wisdom (the topic of this book). I was feeling reasonably successful, but not nearly as wise as other people thought I was, and not nearly as wise as I wanted to be.

A great friend told me several years ago that if he could be granted one wish he would ask for wisdom. I thought he was one of the wisest persons I knew, so his comment intrigued me. It also started me on a ten-year exploration of the sources of wisdom. It involved reading books written by and about wise people of the past and present, and talking and listening to all the wise people I could find. It also involved ten more years of living, making mistakes, and growing. In all, it was a great period of learning that I'm now pleased to share with others. I think all of us want to grow in wisdom.

Wisdom is the result when we learn to make better choices.
                                                    —ERWIN G. HALL

Chapter One

HUMILITY

LIFE IS A LESSON IN HUMILITY.
BE HUMBLE . . . OR BE HUMBLED.

DEFINITIONS

Humility: the quality or state of being humble. Not proud or haughty.

—MERRIAM-WEBSTER

Humility is to make a right estimate of one's self.

—CHARLES SPURGEON

RELATED WORDS/ VIRTUES	OPPOSITE WORDS/ FLAWS
Unassuming	Arrogant
Modest	Proud
Self-effacing	Self-centered

1. Humility

This is the greatest and most useful lesson we can learn: to know ourselves for what we truly are, to admit freely our weaknesses and failings, and to hold a humble opinion of ourselves because of them. Not to dwell on ourselves and always to think well and highly of others is great wisdom.

—THOMAS A'KEMPIS

Think what the world would be like if everyone were a little more humble. Surely it would be a nicer place if we were more willing to admit that we don't know everything, that we have weaknesses, and that we make mistakes. It would be even better if we'd confess that we're wrong and say we're sorry more often. And it would be better yet if we always treated each other with respect and dignity. A little more humility would make the world a much nicer place.

Why is lack of humility such a problem? Because of a basic flaw that we all seem to share—we're too often preoccupied with ourselves. It's the human condition. We come into the world totally dependent upon others for both our survival and our comfort, and we begin thinking that everything revolves around us. In addition, we grow up in a society that reinforces this attitude by constantly reminding us to look out for "number one." The problem with this is that if we all have a "me first" mindset, we end up making life more difficult for others, and ultimately for ourselves.

Another reason lack of humility is a problem is that humility is so often portrayed as a weakness. Many people associate it with being meek and mild—even wimpy. But we have many examples from history that prove just the opposite. Humility is actually a sign of strength, and some of our greatest leaders have proven it. As a history major in college, I studied the lives of hundreds of people who helped shape this country. Many of them were humble. Here are a few of them.

THREE HUMBLE LEADERS

Humility is a visible demonstration of concern ancompassion,
as well as authenticity. Leaders who are to be followed must
be leaders who understand the human condition,
especially their own.

—JOHN BALDONI

Almost all historians agree that Abraham Lincoln was both our greatest president and a remarkable human being. The key to his success was his ability to bring out the best in others. Men of enormous talent and equally enormous egos surrounded him in the White House. Instead of battling them, he acknowledged their talent, stroked their egos, praised their accomplishments, and helped them serve our country in a time of crisis. He was able to do this because he wanted to preserve our country and didn't seek the credit or the accolades. Abraham Lincoln was a humble man.

Historians also rank Harry Truman as one of our greatest presidents. I was so fascinated by Truman's achievements and character, I chose him as the subject of my master's thesis. For more than a year I was consumed by the story of this man who led us through one of the most critical periods in our history. That year culminated in one of the biggest thrills of my life—a week of research among the original documents in the Truman Library in Independence, Missouri, and a personal interview with the great man himself in his private office. We talked at length about momentous events and decisions pertaining to World War II and the postwar period. Without so much as a hint of pride, this highly esteemed president talked about all the people who helped him get the job done. When I returned to school to share the experience with my professor, he asked, "So how was the great Harry Truman?" I answered, "The great Harry Truman is one of the most humble persons I've ever met."

David Packard, one of the greatest and most influential business leaders in our country's history, was also humble. The cofounder of Hewlett-Packard and the winner of several humanitarian awards, Packard was revered by both his colleagues and his competitors, not only for his vision and leadership, but for his kindness, generosity, and humble spirit. As a manager he scorned authoritarian rule and shunned the spotlight. He brought out the best in his coworkers by trusting them and encouraging their creativity, and he gave them credit for the success of the company. Humility is not taught in schools of business and management courses, but David Packard proved that it can be an effective leadership tool. He won the hearts and minds of those around him because of it.

Will the entire world change for the better if one person becomes more humble? No. Will that one person's world change for the better if he or she becomes more humble? Yes. When we become more humble we take some of the focus off ourselves, and become better persons in the process. We become kinder and more caring. And we improve the quality of life—our own and of those around us.

When I wrote the first edition of *Life's Greatest Lessons* in 1990 it contained twenty virtues and principles that I thought were the most basic and necessary for genuine success in life. Humility was not one of them. It would be today. It's chapter one in this book for a very simple reason—I've learned a painful, yet valuable lesson: Be humble, or be humbled.

For everyone who exalts himself will be humbled, and he who humbles himself will be exalted.

—LUKE 14:11

After crosses and losses, men grow humbler and wiser.
—BENJAMIN FRANKLIN

In the process of exploring the relationship between humility and wisdom, I discovered the quotation by Thomas A'Kempis presented at the beginning of this chapter. A'Kempis was a great theologian and philosopher in Europe in the 1400s. He called holding a humble opinion of ourselves "the greatest and most useful lesson we can learn." While this seems inconsistent with the current mores of society, some of the greatest psychologists, philosophers, and theologians of both past and present would support his conclusion. His simple yet profound statement had a major impact on me. So I copied the quotation into my journal directly below my personal mission statement, and I now read both of them every morning before doing anything else. Reading a quote about humility every morning won't turn anyone into a humble person, but it reinforces a powerful idea, keeps a person focused, and helps immensely in the process.

THE ORIGINAL SIN: PRIDE

If pride turned some of the angels into demons, then humility can doubtless make angels out of demons
—ST. JOHN CLIMACUS

Good stories have a way of staying with us for a long time. That's why the best teachers and speakers use them so often. For making an important point, they'll beat a lecture any day. I can still vividly remember a story I was told by Sister Teresita, a wonderful nun who was my third-grade teacher. The story was about the beginning of time when God created heaven and earth. We were spellbound, especially by the part about angels and how glorious Lucifer, the head angel, was. He was God's "main man"—the most beautiful, most powerful, and most intelligent creature in heaven. But Lucifer got carried away with himself. He decided he wanted to be more important than God, and tried to take over. In the battle of angels that ensued, Michael the archangel defeated him. Lucifer was banished from heaven, sent to hell, and became known as Satan, or the Devil. The point of the story was that he committed the first, or original, sin. It was pride. He was too impressed with himself. I remember thinking at the time, "What a dummy! He had a great thing going and then lost all of it. I would never have done anything that stupid."

Sister Teresita followed the Lucifer/Satan story with another downer about Adam and Eve. They had it almost as good as Lucifer did, and they got to live in a place called Paradise. They had everything they could ever want. All they had to do to stay happy and healthy forever was to stay away from one lousy apple tree. But the former Lucifer was still at it. Satan appeared to Eve as a serpent and told her if she'd eat the forbidden fruit she'd become like God and know everything. She convinced Adam of the same thing, they ate it, got caught, and were kicked out of Paradise. This, we were told, was the reason we had to go to school, work, suffer, and eventually die. I can still remember . being totally bummed out by this story. "How could they be so stupid? Why did they have to go and wreck it for all the rest of us? I would have never done that." I was angry at Adam and Eve for years.

I don't mean to make light of either of these stories, but to share my reaction to them from a third-grader's perspective. Also to point out that the stories have stuck with me for more than fifty years. Some people take them literally, and some don't. That's not the issue. The real issue is that they both make their point clearly. That's the reason they've been handed down for many centuries, and probably the reason St. Augustine said, "Pride is the commencement of all sin." Self-centeredness leads to most of our problems.

No one has written more eloquently about pride and its antidote—humility—than C. S. Lewis, the great English novelist and literary scholar. Rather than try to paraphrase his brilliance, I'll let him speak for himself. He wrote the following gems in 1943 in his classic book, *Mere Christianity*. They speak loudly to all of us, regardless of our spiritual convictions.

> *There is no fault which makes a man more unpopular, and no fault which we are more unconscious of in ourselves. And the more we have it in ourselves, the more we dislike it in others.*
>
> *The vice I am talking of is Pride, or Self-Conceit.*
>
> *Nearly all those evils in the world which people put down to greed or selfishness are really far more the result of Pride.*
>
> *It is Pride which has been the chief cause of misery in every nation and every family since the world began.*
>
> *The virtue opposite to it [Pride] . . . is called Humility. If anyone would like to acquire humility, I can, I think, tell him the first step. The first step is to realize that one is proud. And a biggish step, too. At least, nothing whatever can be done before*

*it. If you think you are not conceited, it means you are very
conceited indeed.*

A dear and humble friend recently told me that he wished he
had paid more attention to the pitfalls of pride and the rewards of
humility earlier in life. Don't we all? We usually see pride as someone else's problem, and aren't aware of it in ourselves. Then we gain
a better perspective and realize that everyone has a problem with
pride to some extent. We become more aware of our own pride
when we experience the emotional pain that it often causes for others as well as ourselves. Fortunately, pain can be a great teacher.

It teaches us that when our hearts are in the wrong place, we
often end up with the opposite of what we seek. When we're preoccupied with ourselves, we think mostly about *getting*. But when
we're in that state, the attention, honor, and praise we want don't
seem to come. That's because we unknowingly sabotage ourselves.
We repel people when we're full of ourselves. It's only when we
unselfishly *give,* and are *not* looking out for just ourselves, that the
best things in life come our way.

HUMILITY IN AMERICA?

*When science discovers the center of the universe, a lot of people
will be disappointed to find they are not it.*

—BERNARD BAILY

For hundreds of years in this country, self-centeredness
and self-promotion were considered rude. In fact, they
were appalling to most people. If you were good at
something you kept quiet about it and let others sing your praises.

That was the polite thing to do. David Packard, cited earlier as a model of both humility and strong leadership, said, "You shouldn't gloat about anything you've done; you ought to keep going and find something better to do." This was an opinion shared by many.

But there's been a shift since the days of Packard. Both self-centeredness and gloating are on the increase. We're much more likely to focus on, and glorify, the "self" than we were a few decades back, and in many circles it's become the norm. How did we move from being relatively modest and gracious people to ones who often have a "me first" attitude and think nothing of bragging? Social critics point to a number of recent trends.

One of those critics is Christopher Lasch. In his best-selling book *The Culture of Narcissism,* he says we moved from an "us society" to a "me society." Lasch blames much of this trend on what he calls the "Awareness Movement." He says too many people put too much time and energy into discovering their real selves, and that it eventually led to "self-absorption . . . to the dead end of a narcissistic preoccupation with the self."

There's no doubt that many people did go a bit overboard in trying to become "self-actualized" during the 1970s. I was one of them, and I can understand in hindsight why it's been labeled the "Me Decade." But not all self-examination is bad, and many people benefited from their journeys. There were a number of other significant changes going on that contributed even more to our becoming a less humble society. Here are some of them:

- Proliferation of the media, making it easier to bombard us with reasons to glorify ourselves
- A new thrust in advertising urging us to worship the "self"
- High-profile business leaders' glorifying themselves and their lifestyles
- Brash messages from celebrities in the entertainment world
- Bragging and trash-talking by athletes

TWO POSTER BOYS OF BRAGGADOCIO

People who capture the attention of the media, often because their behavior is outrageous, sometimes become trend-setters. Here are a few examples from two important arenas within our society: sports and business.

1. Muhammad Ali

As I write this, Muhammad Ali is an elderly and disabled former world boxing champion. He's also highly respected for many of his achievements. My point here is not to denigrate him, but to show how he changed the way many athletes behave. Until he came along, good sportsmanship, team play, and gracious winning were considered the norms in athletics. But when a world champion with an electrifying personality claims, "I am the greatest!" things begin to change. When he says later, "It's hard to be humble when you're as great as I am," things change even more.

Ali became world-famous, not only for his achievements in the ring, but for his poetry, predictions, wild antics, humor, and claims of greatness. People either loved him or hated him, but he got their attention. And because he could back up his often outrageous claims, he started a new trend: self-promotion. Suddenly it was acceptable to claim that you were the best, especially if you were good at something. Other athletes followed suit. Bragging and trash-talking your opponent not only increased, but filtered down to college and high-school athletics.

2. Donald Trump

Other celebrities discovered that the more you brag and the more outrageously you act, the more media attention you get. The practice also filtered into the world of big business. A number of CEOs and other executives also became darlings of the media. And some of them became more flamboyant as they garnered more power and attention. Lavish parties and conspicuous possessions were highly publicized. And getting your name out there could only help business. The poster boy of all this was Donald Trump. The more things he plastered his name on, the more the media loved him. He even got his own TV show. Part of his philosophy, expressed in his own words, is: "Toot your own horn." He stated, "Subtlety and modesty are appropriate for nuns and therapists, but if you're in business, you'd better learn to speak up and announce your contributions to the world. No one else will."

I don't mean to imply that every athlete now brags like Ali did or that every executive operates like Trump does. There are still many humble people in both sports and business. But Ali and Trump learned how to play to the media, and received the publicity that comes with it. It's what people see and hear, and many of them conclude that this is what it takes to be successful in any endeavor. Someone once said, "Image is everything." And unfortunately, a large portion of society has bought into that concept.

Obviously, times have changed. Now we're bombarded daily with reminders that we can all be great. We not only can, but should, have it all. We need to have all the cool things, look cool, be cool, and let everyone know we're cool. "If you've got it, flaunt it." More and more people openly brag about their greatness. We see and hear many famous people toot their own horns. These are the superstars everyone seems to admire the most. The media can't get enough of them because they're the coolest of the cool. Why not try to be like them? The message is that we need to be brash and bold in order to succeed.

In spite of all this, there's still hope. I vividly recall a lecture given by one of my professors in college more than forty years ago.

He called it "The Pendulum of History." He said trends come and trends go—in politics, religion, business, fashion, entertainment, and social mores. Some are fads, which flame out quickly, and some are trends, which hang around longer, disappear, and then return later. But, he said, we always end up getting back to the basics—the rock-solid virtues that provide us with stability, a sense of community, and peace of mind. Good character will always be the bedrock of a good person and of a good society.

THE FOUNDATION OF ALL VIRTUES

> *Humility is the solid foundation of all the virtues.*
>
> —CONFUCIUS

> *True humility . . . is the low but deep and firm foundation of all virtues.*
>
> —EDMUND BURKE

Solomon, Buddha, Socrates, and many other wise people throughout the ages make a strong case for pride being the foundation of all the other vices. Whenever we see a copy of the Seven Deadly Sins, pride is always listed first, because it's the starting place for all the others: greed, lust, anger, gluttony, envy, and sloth. Since humility is the opposite of pride, a strong argument can be made for its being the foundation of all the other virtues.

> *The test of a truly great man or woman is their humility. I do not mean by humility, doubt of their own power. But really great people have a curious feeling that the greatness is not in them, but through them.*
>
> —JOHN RUSKIN

Again, I'll say that humility is not a sign of weakness, but one of strength. People can be highly successful in any endeavor, be strong and effective leaders, and still remain humble. They may not appear on TV and in the newspapers much, but we all know people like this. More important, we admire them. There have also been a lot of excellent examples throughout history. I cited Abraham Lincoln, Harry Truman, and David Packard earlier as a models of both humility and strong leadership. Think also of the legacy left by these leaders: Benjamin Franklin, Albert Einstein, Harriet Tubman, Mohatma Gandhi, Clara Barton, Albert Schweitzer, Martin Luther King, Jr., Mother Teresa, and many others who have shown us that we don't have to beat our own drums in order to accomplish something of significance.

WHAT DOES HUMILITY LOOK LIKE?

The key to acquiring any great virtue is to first see it in others. That helps us understand not only what it is, but what it looks like. What does humility look like? What do humble people do, and what do they not do?

Four Things Humble People *Don't* Do

1. Humble people don't think they know everything.

> It wasn't until quite late in life that I discovered how easy it is to say, "I don't know."
>
> —SOMERSET MAUGHAM

2. Humble people don't think they're always right.

> *Nobody stands taller than those willing to stand corrected.*
> —WILLIAM SAFIRE

> *Pride is concerned with who is right. Humility is concerned with what is right.*
> —EZRA TAFT BENSON

3. Humble people don't brag.

> *What kills a skunk is the publicity it gives itself.*
> —ABRAHAM LINCOLN

> *When someone sings his own praises, he always gets the tune too high.*
> —MARY H. WALDRIP

4. Humble people don't judge others.

> *I look only to the good qualities of men. Not being faultless myself, I won't presume to probe into the faults of others.*
> —MAHATMA GANDHI

> *Do not judge, or you too will be judged. For in the same way you judge others, you will be judged, and with the measure you use, it will be measured to you. Why do you look at the speck in your brother's eye and pay no attention to the plank in your own eye?*
> —MATTHEW 7:1–3

Four Things Humble People Consistently Do

1. Humble people treat others with respect.

> *Humility and respect go hand in hand.*
> —PAUL H. BORISOFF

> *Treat other people exactly as you would like to be treated by them.*
> —MATTHEW 7:12

2. Humble people are thankful.

> *Prideful people never have enough. Humble people appreciate what they have.*
> —JEAN DREYFUS

> *It is not how much we have, but how much we enjoy.*
> —CHARLES SPURGEON

3. Humble people are genuine.

> *Pride makes us artificial and humility makes us real.*
> —THOMAS MERTON

> *I have three precious things which I hold fast and prize. The first is gentleness; the second is frugality; the third is humility, which keeps me from putting myself before others.*
> —LAO-TZU

4. Humble people want to learn and become better.

Humility is an approach to life that says "I don't have all the
answers and I want your contributions."

—JOHN BALDONI

Being prepared to set aside old notions and be taught by life
is learning humility.

—MICHAEL MCGINNIS

There are four other qualities humble people demonstrate:
patience, empathy, giving, and forgiveness—the topics of the next
four chapters.

THE PARADOX OF HUMILITY

When we become aware of our humility, we've lost it.

—ANONYMOUS

There's something very tricky and elusive about humility. If we think we have it, we don't. In the same way,
if we think we don't have a problem with pride, we do.
To make that point, here's an e-mail message I sent to my
wife, Cathy, on the day I completed this chapter: "I just finished
the first chapter of the new book. It is absolutely fabulous! In fact,
it's so good people will now recognize me as one of the greatest
writers of all time. It's about humility." Then I added a few more
lines: "I finally have this humility thing down. After working so
hard on all this reading and writing, I can now say with great pride
that I'm a genuinely humble person. I already have the title of my
next book—*Humility and How I Mastered It.*"

The truth is that none of us is without pride and none of us is completely humble. The real key is acknowledging this while working to reduce pride and grow in humility. As stated in the preface, I write about humility, not because I have it, but because I know I need to work on it. Drawing on the wisdom of so many others has been helpful. I hope it helps you, too.

Life is a long lesson in humility.

—John Matthew Barrie

Chapter Two

PATIENCE

Think before you act. Patience is the first step toward understanding and peacefulness.

DEFINITIONS

Patience: the capacity, habit, or fact of being patient. Not hasty or impetuous.

—Merriam-Webster

Patience is quiet hope and trust, expecting things to turn out all right. Patience is being calm and tolerant when difficult things happen.

—The Virtues Project Educator's Guide

RELATED WORDS/ VIRTUES

Self-control
Serenity
Inner strength

OPPOSITE WORDS/ FLAWS

Impatience
Irritation
Intolerance

2. PATIENCE

EVERY DAY IS A TEST OF PATIENCE

*Every day brings some exasperation—some need, small or great,
that forces us to exercise patience. Patience is just part of the
equipment we need if we are going to cope with life.*

—JIM LONG

Some funny things happened on the way to writing a chapter about patience. I do quite a bit of reading before writing, and it always begins with a search for books on the topic. After finding one on the Internet about patience that looked like it might be particularly helpful, I called my local bookstore to see if it was in stock. I gave the man the title, and he said, "Hold on." I did for more than a few minutes, which seemed like a half hour. When he came back on the line, he asked me if I had the author's name. I did, and gave it to him. Again, he told me, "Hold on." This wait was longer, and seemed more like an hour. Finally, he came back on again to tell me, "I'm having trouble finding that book in our system. Do you have the ISBN number?" I did, and gave it to him. And, of course, he told me for the third time, "Hold on." Another wait of more than a few minutes, and this one seemed like at least an hour and a half. Why does time go so much slower when we're put on hold?

All kinds of questions were running through my head while waiting: How many days has he been working at the store? Why wouldn't a big chain bookstore like this one be able to give me an immediate answer? What was taking so long? Then the irony crept in. How patient would I be under the same circumstances if I wasn't writing about that very topic? Probably not as patient as I'd been so far. But the test wasn't over. The man came back on the line to tell me that with the title, name of the author, and the ISBN number, he still couldn't find the book "in the system." He then informed me that he was turning it all over to another person at the store, but that person was currently busy, so naturally, he asked me again to "hold on." I think this other person must have been having lunch or taking a little siesta, because it seemed like at least two hours before he came on the line. He then politely told me something I already knew: "Something seems to be wrong with the system." I resisted the urge to comment on either "the system" or the amount of time I had wasted on the phone. He also informed me that he was "too busy at the moment" to look on the shelves for me. Maybe he needed to finish his nap.

Since the bookstore is only two miles from my home, I thought I would drive down and take a look. Along the way I got stuck on a residential street because someone was trying to back a truck into a driveway, was having trouble getting it in straight, and was blocking traffic both ways. I tried to back up so I could turn around and go another way, but there were already three cars behind me. My normal five-minute drive to the bookstore took about twenty minutes. When I got there, there were already eight people in line at customer service, and each one seemed to be looking for the most rare book on the planet. I was thinking, "This can't really be happening." But it was. When I finally got to the counter, "the system" was working fine, and the clerk politely told me that the book was not in stock, but that she could get it for me in two weeks. Again, I resisted my urge, which was to scream out, "I want that book on patience, and I want it NOW!" I was feeling that I really, really needed it at this point.

So I headed home with full confidence that the guy in the truck had everything straightened out and that the road was clear.

But little did I know that the test *still* wasn't over. I followed another car out of the parking lot and headed for home. The elderly man in front of me was taking the same route, but was traveling at a much more "leisurely" pace than I had planned on. We were in a twenty-five-mile-per-hour zone, but he apparently wanted to be extra cautious. For the next several minutes, which seemed more like two and half hours, he drove between eighteen and twenty miles per hour. And of course, it seemed much slower than that to the guy behind him—me. I was sure he would turn off on a side street, but he didn't. He went all the way to the street I live on, as if he was leading the way, and asking me, "So you want to write a chapter about patience, do you? Well, how do you like these apples?"

Finally, I arrived back home, got myself comfortable, turned on the computer, and began once again to write about the wonders of patience. Then the power went out . . . and stayed out for the rest of the day. The next morning the power was back on, but five minutes into writing . . . my computer went down. Whoever said God doesn't have a sense of humor? On the other hand, maybe God was just being helpful, and he was saying, "Let me give you a little help on that chapter. Let me humble you a little and test your own patience before you start telling other people about what a great virtue it is."

I tell this story for two reasons. First, because it seems almost comical that this series of tests would occur while I was preparing to write about patience. And the timing was perfect. It taught me something of great value and put me in just the right mindset. I had just demonstrated more patience than I thought was humanly possible (for me, at least). And in the process I became convinced that anyone else could do the same. Patience is, indeed, a mindset, and being able to laugh at the absurdity of our trials is a big help. Second, this series of events provided a perfect example of the type of tests we endure daily. I'm sure that you can recall similar experiences in your own life. As Jim Long says in the quote at the beginning of this section, patience is "part of the equipment we need if we are going to cope with life."

PATIENCE IN A HIGH-SPEED SOCIETY?

We're all suffering from "hurry sickness."

—JAMES GLEICK

There are two things that are most likely to make people struggle with patience. The first is our genetic makeup. Some of us come from a gene pool that has a lot of "calm, cool, and collected" in it. Patience comes more naturally. Others of us come from a gene pool that has a lot of "wham, bam, slam" in it, along with a few too many fits of rage. If you come from this latter pool (as I do), patience is more difficult to acquire, but still very much possible. Regardless of personality type, the greatest challenge we all face is the microwave society in which we live. We're bombarded daily with messages that have these words and phrases in them:

fast	quick	high-speed	rapid
express	swift	sudden	prompt
immediate	at once	without delay	in a flash
now	in no time	lightning-like	momentarily

But it isn't just the messages that get into our heads, it's what we experience on a day-to-day basis. At home, all we have to do to turn on the TV, change the channel, heat our food, open the garage door, dry the clothes, wash the dishes, or make a phone call is push a single button. At work we're encouraged (pushed) to get our assignments done quickly and to become proficient at "multitasking." In sports they're trying to figure out how they can "speed up" the games. In places of worship the pastor carefully watches the length of the sermon because people get fidgety and want to leave. They probably want to go out for a bite to eat at a fast-food restaurant.

So what do you do if you have a "hurry" gene in your lineage, work in a high-stress job, commute every day, and have kids at home? You learn to become more patient.

PATIENCE IS A VIRTUE AND AN ART . . . AND IT *CAN* BE LEARNED.

Patience can be learned, and great patience allows us to accept our own humanity with all our imperfections.
— MARY ELLEN PATTERSON

Learn the art of patience. Apply discipline to your thoughts when they become anxious . . . . Impatience breeds anxiety, fear, discouragement, and failure. Patience creates confidence, decisiveness, and a rational outlook, which eventually leads to success.
— BRIAN ADAMS

Ask one hundred people if they'd like to have more patience, and more than ninety-five of them will tell you "yes." And even if you don't ask why, most of them will tell you anyway. Fully aware of my own lack of patience, I thought I'd ask others how they were doing. I asked literally hundreds of people on airplanes and in my workshops. Their answers surprised me. It seems like almost everyone feels a need for more patience. A dear friend, one of the most humble, kind, and gentle persons I know, told me recently that he was praying for and working on becoming more patient. While it made me feel a little better knowing that I'm not alone, it also reminded me just how much work I have to do in this area. I'd be a rich man if someone gave me a dollar for every time I was impatient. In fact, I'd be pretty well off if I only got a quarter.

Most of us were taught as children that "patience is a virtue." It is. It's also a sign of strength. We all admire people who manage to consistently show restraint and stay calm when things around them get chaotic. Unfortunately, what most of us were *not* taught was how to become more patient ourselves. Just being told that it's a virtue isn't enough. That's why so many of us continue to struggle. Studies on personality tell us that some types of people are calm by nature, and therefore, more likely to be patient. But what about the rest of us—the other types? Fortunately, there's hope. The most important point to be made here is that patience *can* be learned, even by someone with a hard-charging Type A personality—like me.

Although I read several excellent books and articles about patience in preparing to write this chapter, something much simpler proved to be of greater value. I talked at length with the four most patient people I know. I asked each of them how they had developed it. Their initial answers were almost identical: "I learned the hard way." Although they had different stories about how they'd developed patience, the principles they'd learned were the same:

- Patience starts with feeling a genuine need for it.
- Patience requires strong desire and motivation.
- Patience is hard work, especially at the beginning.
- Patience requires practice, practice, practice.
- Patience becomes easier as it becomes a habit.
- Patience enriches every aspect of life.

All four of these people asked me if I thought of myself as an impatient person. And each of them received a resounding "YES." They also asked me if I had ever learned to be patient in any areas of my life. I laughed and said that I *had* to learn to be patient in my teaching career. I couldn't have survived thirty-five years of being with 150 teenagers all day without a lot of patience. I'd also learned to be patient while traveling. Things often go wrong, and the more upset one gets, the worse the experience becomes. I've learn to be prepared and to make the most of each situation. My mentors then made a simple point—if you can learn to be patient in these circumstances, you can learn to be patient in *all* circumstances. They were right.

Of the many books I found on the subject, the one I liked best was *The Power of Patience,* by M. J. Ryan. The author is, by her own admission, a "speeded-up, Type A, overachieving middle age woman." She did extensive reading and research on patience, and then applied the principles to her own life. Her book is both easy to read and heartwarming, with a special emphasis on the many rewards of becoming more patient: better health, better relationships, better decisions, better lives. She says if she can do it, anyone can. She gives us the keys to develop more patience by telling us that "with the right attitudes and a bit of practice, we can learn to harness the power of patience in our lives. . . . It's a combination of motivation (wanting to), awareness (paying attention to our inner landscape), and cultivation (practicing)."

THE "BIG FIVE" OF ROUTINE ANNOYANCES ...AND HOW TO DEAL WITH THEM

In a single day we can be faced with countless irritations.
—CHUCK GALLOZZI

"What routine occurrences—other than dealing with people—annoy you and test your patience the most?" This is a question I asked hundreds of people while preparing to write this chapter. It's amazing how cooperative people are when you tell them you're doing research for a book. It makes everyone asked feel like an authority, and they're more than willing to make their expertise on the subject known. There was nothing surprising about their answers. The five mentioned most frequently are the ones that put us all to the test on a regular basis. Here are the "Big Five":

1. Waiting in line
2. Driving a car
3. Using a computer
4. Being put on hold
5. Traveling by air

Although I only asked for the general categories of annoyances, almost everyone who answered felt compelled to give me detailed examples of their tales of woe. Since we all have our own stories in both these and other areas of frustration, it would serve no purpose to retell them here. There is one thing, however, that they all have in common, and is worth mentioning. In all cases, the people telling the stories proved a point: They were "victims of circumstances" because they hadn't learned to develop patience.

Indeed it appears that the faster things go, the less patience we
are able to muster. This is a problem because life inevitably has
a certain degree of delay in the form of lines, traffic jams, and
automated message machines.

—M. J. RYAN

The single most important thing in learning to develop
patience is to understand that it's a mindset, an attitude. Next is to
realize that all attitudes are choices. I thought this topic was so
important I devoted two chapters to it in *Life's Greatest Lessons.*
One of these chapters is about the fact that we live by choice, not
by chance, and the other presents the idea that attitude is a
choice—the most important one you'll ever make. If patience is an
attitude, and attitude is a choice, it logically follows that patience
is a choice. If practiced regularly, it can also become a habit, one
that can greatly enrich our lives.

When we were young, we were taught to "count to ten"
before doing or saying anything rash when we became irritated.
It actually does work, but people rarely use it. Or they count to
ten in two seconds so they can unleash their rage. There are other
simple methods of dealing with impatience, and they're even
more effective than counting to any number. If you start with the
premise that patience is an attitude and a choice—something you
have total control over—then these suggestions should be helpful:

1. Be prepared: Expect at least some things to go wrong
and expect at least a few delays. If you start every day this
way, you won't get thrown for a loss when one comes along.
You'll be ready. If you don't have any glitches or delays, then
be delighted that you were so fortunate.
2. Ask yourself this question: "If I allow this incident to

get me upset and angry, will I make it better . . . or worse?"
You already know the answer.

3. Give yourself a pep talk: Far more effective than
counting to ten is saying something specific and positive to
yourself about the situation. Example: "I can handle this. It's
just another test of my patience."

4. Have a strategy: Since these annoyances are inevitable,
have a plan for making the most of each situation.Examples:
When you're stuck in a line, strike up a conversation with
your fellow sufferers. You might meet someone interesting.
When you're stuck in the car, have a good book-on-tape
available. You might even be able to find one on patience.
When you're stuck in an airport or on an airplane, always
have something good to read. Or go shopping or watch a
game in the bar.

THE BIGGEST CHALLENGE: PATIENCE WITH PEOPLE

What is wrong with people? They can be so exasperating!
—PHOEBE BUFFET ON *FRIENDS*

I was in a restaurant recently and overheard a woman say
to the person she was with, "People—they can be so exasperating!" It was almost the same thing I'd heard Phoebe
says on *Friends* a few nights before. Come to think of it, I've heard
that comment many times . . . and know I've made the same comment a few times myself, as in, "What is *wrong* with people?" The
challenging part is that everywhere we go, there they are—other
people! Think of the long list: spouses, kids at home, other people's
kids, relatives, friends, coworkers, fellow travelers, drivers, shoppers,

cell phone talkers, store employees, neighbors, and so on. Why can't they all be quiet, conscientious, hard-working, efficient, friendly, polite, and understanding? Maybe because they're a lot like us. They have weaknesses, they have bad days, they're often in a hurry, and they're trying to do too many things at one time. They need our patience, just like at times when we need theirs.

I'm really glad that my mom has always been so patient with me. I was fortunate that my teachers and coaches and pastors also showed so much patience. I'm happy that my dearest friends accept my shortcomings and have been patient with me so many times. I'm very appreciative to have been blessed for many years with colleagues who were both understanding and patient with me. And I'm thankful for the numerous times my students were patient and put up with my bad moments. I'm lucky to work with a publisher and an editor who patiently help me deal with the many frustrations of writing. I feel privileged to have three sons who often demonstrated extraordinary patience with their dad's mistakes. And I'm particularly grateful that my wife, Cathy, is so often more patient with me than I deserve. In short, I'm fortunate to have had so many people in my life who've patiently tolerated my flaws.

How about you? Is your story much different? I doubt that it is. Think of all the wonderful people who've been kind, understanding, and tolerant when you were being less than your best. Where would you be without them? Doesn't it make you want to work on becoming more patient with the people around you?

How can we expect to have others accept our weakness unless we are willing to accept theirs? Patience, then, is about respect for others.

—CHUCK GALLOZZI

SEVEN EXPERTS ON LEARNING, ACHIEVEMENT, AND PATIENCE

If I have ever made any valuable discoveries, it has been owing more to patient attention than to any other talent.

—ISAAC NEWTON

I think and think for months and years. Ninety-nine times the conclusion is false. The hundreth time I am right. It's not that I'm so smart, it's just that I stay with problems longer.

—ALBERT EINSTEIN

Genius is nothing but a greater aptitude for patience.

—BENJAMIN FRANKLIN

Everything comes to him who hustles while he waits.

—THOMAS EDISON

Genius is eternal patience.

—MICHELANGELO

Patience and fortitude conquer all things.

—RALPH WALDO EMERSON

Patience and perseverance have a magical effect before which difficulties and obstacles vanish.

—JOHN QUINCY ADAMS

Above are the names of seven rather distinguished and well-known gentlemen, to say the least. Two scientists who have made profound discoveries, the most prolific inventor of all time, a primary architect of our country's democratic system, an artist ranked with the greats of all time, one of America's most insightful writers, and a highly respected president of the United States. All are known for their exceptional achievements, and all have been called geniuses. Yet, in their own words, there would be no genius and no achievement without patience. Keep in mind that it was Edison who defined genius as "one percent inspiration and ninety-nine percent perspiration." His own perspiration came from long, long hours of hard work.

Whether it's the seven notable historical figures listed above or many of today's leaders in business, the arts, science, athletics, law, service, or ministry, the road to learning and achievement remains the same. No matter how many times the media tell us that there's a "quick and easy" way to get anything we want, we need to remind ourselves that nothing worthwhile has ever been achieved without the three Ps—perseverance, persistence, and patience.

PATIENCE ALL THE TIME? NO

Patience has its limits. Take it too far, and it's cowardice.
—GEORGE JACKSON

I don't want to imply that patience is the solution to every problem. It isn't. This chapter is about the times when being patient will help us deal more effectively with most of those problems, whether it's a difficult person, an unexpected delay, or a mechanical breakdown. There are other situations that not only don't call for patience, but don't warrant it. We should not be patient with crime, cruelty, extreme rudeness, or infringement upon our rights. These occurrences call on us to stand up, and they require tact and diplomacy, not patience.

Patience should also not be confused with laziness. Sitting around waiting for good things to happen is not patience. It's either ignorance or laziness, or both. Patience is working hard while waiting for our efforts to pay off.

THE ULTIMATE REWARD

For the more we cultivate patience, the happier and more peaceful we are, even if things don't always turn out the way we want.

—M. J. RYAN

Working on this chapter has been the most enlightening writing experience I've ever had. While writing this chapter, my patience has been challenged more than at any time I can remember. Yet this very impatient person showed more patience than ever before. Why? Simply because I was writing about the importance of patience, knew I needed to work harder on developing it, and concluded that there'd never be a better time to "practice what I preach."

What's surprised me the most is not only the sense of calm and peace that comes over you when you're practicing patience, but how long it stays with you afterward. In her book about patience, M. J. Ryan says, "Indeed, the longer I study and practice patience, the more I've come to see that it is a crucial factor in whether we have satisfying lives or not." She also points out that patience helps us make wiser choices and makes us more loving toward other people. In short, patience makes us better persons. Ryan also sees a relationship between patience and wisdom, and says the greatest rewards are "healthier relationships, higher-quality work, and peace of mind." This writer is convinced that she's correct. No wonder Solomon, the ancient sages of the east, and the other great philosophers throughout history have advised us to be patient.

Patience is the companion of wisdom.

—ST. AUGUSTINE

Chapter Three

EMPATHY

Sensitivity toward others takes
the spotlight off ourselves. Be
caring and compassionate.

DEFINITIONS

*Empathy: the action of understanding, being aware of, being
sensitive to, and vicariously experiencing the feelings, thoughts,
and experiences of another.*

—Merriam-Webster

*Empathy is the ability to read and understand people and be
in tune with or resonate with others.*

—Christel Broederlow

RELATED WORDS/ VIRTUES	OPPOSITE WORDS/ FLAWS
Compassion	Self-centeredness
Understanding	Insensitivity
Caring	Heartlessness

3. Empathy

EMPATHY: THE FOUNDATION OF GOODNESS

The roots of morality are to be found in empathy.
—MARTIN L. HOFFMAN, PH.D.

In doing research on empathy before writing this chapter, I kept bumping into other related words: understanding, thoughtfulness, caring, compassion, sympathy, kindness, and other virtues that remind us about the goodness of which we're capable. One of the things I noticed is that several writers use the terms "empathy" and "compassion" almost interchangeably, as if they mean the same thing. They don't, so it might be helpful to distinguish between the two before going on. Psychologists who have studied both traits not only make a clear distinction between them, they have concluded that empathy is the starting block. It's necessary not only for compassion, but for all other forms of kindness.

EMPATHY. It is the ability to vicariously put ourselves into another person's position and feel what he or she is feeling. These feelings can be ones of great joy or sadness, or anything in between. Empathy is defined in the *Encyclopedia Brittanica* as: "The ability to imagine oneself in another's place and understand the other's feelings, desires, ideas, and actions." The term comes from the Greek word *empatheia*, which means "feeling into," and the German word *einfuhlung*, which means "in-feeling," and is closely related to sympathy. It was first used in the United States in the 1920s by psychologist Edward Titchener because he wanted a word that was distinct from sympathy. It became an important word in counseling because lack of empathy is a major cause of breakdowns in communication and relationships.

COMPASSION. It is a sense of shared suffering, usually combined with a desire to reduce or alleviate it. Compassion is defined in *Webster's Third International Dictionary* as: "The feeling, or emotion, when a person is moved by the suffering or distress of another, and by the desire to relieve it." Its origins are found in the Latin words *cum* (with) and *patior* (to suffer). Probably the person who has written the most about compassion is the Dalai Lama. In his book *The Art of Happiness,* he says, "It is a mental attitude based on the wish for others to be free of their suffering and is associated with a sense of commitment, responsibility, and respect towards the other." People like the Dalai Lama, Mother Teresa, Desmond Tutu, Albert Schweitzer, Nelson Mandela, and Jimmy Carter are well known for their compassion, and have devoted a good part of their lives to alleviating the suffering of others. But we don't have to be famous or win the Nobel Peace Prize to show compassion. There are opportunities around us almost every day of our lives.

The main difference between empathy and compassion is that empathy is a much broader term. It has to do with understanding the full range of feelings in another person. That's why it's the foundation of so many virtues. Compassion is a narrower term with a focus on the suffering of others and the desire to do something about it. It is empathy that initially helps us to be less self-centered and to understand what's going on inside other people. As it develops we become more caring, compassionate, and giving. In other words, we become better persons while finding more meaning, purpose, and joy in our lives.

> *The heart of the person before you is a mirror. See there your own form.*
>
> —SOCRATES

Until he extends his circle of compassion to all living things,
man will not himself find peace.

—ALBERT SCHWEITZER

EMPATHY, CHARACTER, AND COMMUNICATION

O Divine Master, grant that I may not so much seek . . . to be
understood as to understand.

—ST. FRANCIS OF ASSISI

One of the most widely read books of all time is Stephen R. Covey's classic, *The 7 Habits of Highly Effective People*. Asked many times in interviews which of the seven habits is the most difficult to practice, he answers that number five is, by far. That habit is "Seek first to understand, then to be understood." Why is it the most challenging? Because it's the opposite of what usually happens when two or more people are talking to each other. The more natural tendency is to want the other persons to understand us, and the more we focus on that aim, the less we try to understand them.

When other people talk to us, especially when it's about some kind of problem, we have a natural tendency to want to rush in and help them fix it with our advice. What we don't try to do is see the problem from the other person's perspective. Covey points out that "we often fail to take the time to diagnose, to really, deeply understand the problem first." He says learning to see the problem as the other person does, to understand what the other person is feeling, is one of the most valuable social skills we could ever develop: "Communication is the most important skill in life."

Covey also reminds us that our ability to empathize with others is a reflection of our character—the type of person we truly are.

It's not something that can be hidden or disguised. It's something that always shows through. In Covey's words, "Your character is constantly radiating, communicating. From it, in the long run, I come to instinctively trust or distrust you and your efforts with me." He points out that the only way two or more people can effectively interact is to experience authentic understanding among them. This is far more likely to take place when empathy is embedded in the character ethic of the people involved.

EMPATHY AND LISTENING

When people talk, listen completely. Most people never listen.

—ERNEST HEMINGWAY

If we were supposed to talk more than we listen, we would have two mouths and one ear.

—MARK TWAIN

During my thirty-five years as a public-school teacher, I worked with nine different principals. One of the most interesting was a man we'll call John. He was a dedicated educator and had a big heart and a good sense of humor. He was generally popular with the staff in the beginning, but soon became the cause of great frustration. The reason was simple: He didn't listen. After he'd been at the school for a semester, we were asked to fill out an evaluation of his performance, and he was to report the results to us at a midyear faculty meeting. When the time came, this is what he said: "I guess things are going OK. The only thing a lot of people wanted me to know is that I don't listen to them. That's no big deal. My wife has been telling me that for thirty years."

Sadly, he didn't see the importance of listening, and it seriously hampered his effectiveness. Teachers became more and more frustrated, and many began placing books and articles on good listening skills in his mailbox in the faculty workroom. He thought it was a joke—but it wasn't. He said, "You can stop putting those things in my box now. I get the point." But he didn't get the point, and we were all convinced that he never read any of the material. He lasted only three years, primarily because the teachers became increasingly upset, and complained loudly and frequently to the superintendent.

I shared this story with the adult students in my Communication in Organizations class at the University of San Francisco. Most of them laughed, and concluded that things weren't much different in education than they were at their places of work. It seemed as though everyone in the class had one or more similar stories. One student observed, "Most bosses think their job is to talk, not to listen. Most of them need to get some training or do some reading about the importance of listening. It would make them a lot more effective."

Since the early 1980s there have been numerous books and articles written about the importance of good communication. Many of them are outstanding. If you were to read all of them, and were then asked to summarize the main points, you would probably come up with these five:

1. GOOD COMMUNICATION STARTS WITH GOOD LISTENING. Everyone has a need to be heard. Good listening not only acknowledges the other person, it promotes better understanding, reduces the chance for conflict, and improves relationships in any setting.

2. GOOD LISTENING REQUIRES EMPATHY. There are a number of techniques, such as "active listening" and "reflective listening," which have been published and taught in workshops and seminars. The problem is that they often come off as "gimmicky," and sometimes insulting. Genuine listening begins with empathy, which means listening with the primary intent of truly understanding the other person.

3. Listening with empathy is hard work. Most people think listening comes naturally to us, but it doesn't. Hearing comes naturally, but listening is a skill that has to be developed. Like any other skill, it requires hard work and practice. The hardest part is training ourselves to focus on the needs and feelings of the other person.

4. Good listening is done with our eyes and our hearts. We hear with our ears. We listen with our total being. Empathic listening begins with eye contact. It's the most important nonverbal signal we can send that says, "I'm listening and I'm interested." Good listening comes from the heart.

5. Good listening makes people feel important. In Dale Carnegie's classic 1932 book *How to Win Friends and Influence People,* he says there is no more important social skill than making other people feel important. One of the most basic needs of all human beings is to feel significant, to feel appreciated, to feel that we matter. Nothing does this better than good listening.

EMPATHY AND EMOTIONAL INTELLIGENCE

Much evidence testifies that people who are emotionally adept—who know and manage their own feelings well, and

who read and deal effectively with other people's feelings—are
at an advantage in any domain of life. . . . Empathy . . . is the
fundamental "people skill."

—DANIEL GOLEMAN

Every once in a while a book comes along that changes the way we think. M. Scott Peck's *The Road Less Traveled* did it in 1978 and Covey's book on the seven habits did it in 1989. In 1995 it was Daniel Goleman's turn, when his brilliant book *Emotional Intelligence* was published. As it states on the cover, it is a "groundbreaking book that redefines what it means to be smart." Goleman himself says that emotional intelligence—EQ—can matter more than IQ. As Howard Gardner, the Harvard psychologist who developed the theory of multiple intelligences, has pointed out, "Many people with IQs of 160 work for people with IQs of 100, if the former have poor interpersonal intelligence and the latter have a high one."

Throughout his book, Goleman frequently refers to empathy as an essential trait in people who are emotionally intelligent. In tests with more than seven thousand people throughout the world, it was found that people with empathy proved to be "better adjusted emotionally, more popular, more outgoing, and—perhaps not surprising—more sensitive." He also points out that having the ability to understand how other people feel can help us in all walks of life: friendship, romance, parenting, teaching, coaching, sales, managing, counseling, ministering, and so on. In his conclusion, Goleman says there's an old-fashioned word for the body of skills that emotional intelligence represents: *character.*"

As a teacher who's been deeply involved in the character education movement for several years, I have the opportunity to visit schools all over the country. I see proof that we *can* help young people of all ages develop empathy—and the results are heartwarming. The kids in these schools are nicer to each other and more polite to staff members. Together, they create a caring community, a better atmosphere for both teaching and learning.

TEACHING EMPATHY TO OUR KIDS

To educate a person in mind and not in morals is to educate a menace to society.

—THEODORE ROOSEVELT

Although many people think it started in the early 1990s, character education is not a new idea. In fact, it's as old as education itself. Going as far back as the ancient Greeks, education has always had two main goals. One was to help our children increase in knowledge so they would have the skills and understanding necessary to function in the world. The other goal, which was equally important, was to raise good citizens. This was accomplished by helping young people develop positive character traits. In the United States character development was an integral part of the educational system, both public and private, from colonial days through the end of the 1950s. Due to a wide range of dramatic changes in our society over the next thirty years, character education declined dramatically. Because so many parents and educators saw the need for its return, it made a strong comeback in the 1990s, and continues to grow.

The flagship book of this revival is *Educating for Character: How Our Schools Can Teach Respect and Responsibility,* by Dr. Thomas Lickona. Early in the book, Dr. Lickona tells about an experience he had in the late 1980s while in Japan at an international conference on moral education. He said representatives from fifteen countries all expressed the same worries: "Everyone is concerned about the breakdown of the family; everyone is concerned about the negative impact of television on children; everyone is concerned about the growing self-centeredness, materialism, and delinquency they see among their young." He concludes with these words: "*Not* to equip the young with a moral sense is a grave ethical failure on the part of any society."

The good news is that the character education movement has made a strong comeback, and many communities, places of worship, businesses, service organizations, governments, schools, and parents have bought into it. And there are more dynamic leaders, organizations, conferences, and outstanding resources available than ever before. The movement focuses on virtues such as the six "pillars" of Character Counts! Organization founded by Michael Josephson: respect, responsibility, fairness, caring, trustworthiness, and citizenship. These and all the other virtues that are extolled have the same foundation—empathy.

While working on this chapter, I got a call from one of my former students who had become an elementary-school teacher. She wanted us to get together because she had something exciting to share, so we met a few nights later for dinner. Her good news was that a character education program had been implemented in her school, and she felt it had greatly improved the quality of life for both the kids and the staff members. "Everyone is so much nicer now," she said, "even the teachers to each other!" They had begun their program by teaching empathy. Her third-graders had never even heard the word before, but now they were practicing it daily. Tied to it were respect, caring, compassion, understanding, tolerance, and sympathy. No wonder she was excited! Dr. Michele Borba is a parent, former classroom teacher, author, and one of the leading advocates of character education—in both our homes and our schools. In her book *Building Moral Intelligence,* she explains "the seven essential virtues that teach kids to do the right things." The first of the seven is empathy, the virtue upon which the other six depend. She calls it "the core moral emotion" because it's the one that helps our children become sensitive to the needs and feelings of others, and ultimately helps them do what is right. The other six virtues are conscience, self-control, respect, kindness, tolerance, and fairness.

Dr. Borba offers several practical steps parents and teachers can take to nurture empathy in children. The most important one is to model it in the home and in the school. Another is to emphasize the rewards of empathy—show how it improves understanding and relationships. She also strongly urges parents to regulate what their kids are watching and listening to in order to protect them from harmful images. She says the best opportunities to teach empathy are not planned—"they just happen." This is what educators call "a teachable moment." Opportunities to teach and model empathy appear every day. We owe it to our kids and to ourselves to teach them this important virtue.

THE REWARDS OF EMPATHY

When I started the reading and research phase of writing this chapter, I understood clearly what empathy was, and knew three other essential things about it: 1) It's a wonderful quality to have, 2) all good people have it, 3) I needed more of it. The best part is not only can empathy be learned at any age, it can be increased at any age. I wrote earlier that writing the chapter on patience was an enlightening experience. The same has happened here. It would be impossible to read through the findings of so many experts and not come to this conclusion:

Empathy is one of the most important qualities a human being can have.

Here are some of ways in which the development of empathy can enrich our lives and the lives of the people around us:

- It improves our relationships with the opposite sex.
- It improves our relationships with the same sex.
- It strengthens marriages and families.
- It makes people better spouses, parents, teachers, friends, colleagues, counselors, pastors, doctors, nurses, caregivers, and leaders of all kinds.
- It enhances our communication skills, especially listening.
- It helps us understand and practice the Golden Rule.
- It helps us become more moral and ethical.
- It makes other people feel better about themselves.
- It makes us feel better about ourselves.
- It increases our emotional intelligence.
- It makes us more caring and compassionate, kinder and gentler.
- It helps us become more patient, understanding, and forgiving.
- It earns the respect of other people.
- It makes us happier.
- It makes us better persons.

Empathy shines its light on our deepest needs, never allowing us to forget that our very survival depends on our ability to accurately understand and sensitively respond to each other.

—Arthur P. Ciaramicoli, Ph.D.

Chapter Four

GIVING

IT REALLY IS BETTER TO GIVE THAN
TO RECEIVE. HELP OTHERS WHILE
HELPING YOURSELF.

DEFINITIONS

*Give: to make a present of; to put into the possession of
another for his use; to commit to another as a trust or
responsibility.*

—MERRIAM-WEBSTER

*I have come to believe that giving and receiving are really the
same. Giving and receiving—not giving and taking.*

—JOYCE GRENFELL

RELATED WORDS/ VIRTUES	OPPOSITE WORDS/ FLAWS
Loving	Selfish
Helpful	Uncaring
Generous	Stingy

4. Giving

WE HAVE IT BACKWARDS—GIVING COMES FIRST

*It's a universal law—we have to give before we get. We must
plant the seeds before we reap the harvest. The more we sow, the
more we reap. And in giving to others, we find ourselves blessed.
The law works to give us back more than we have sown. The
giver's harvest is always full.*

—WYNN DAVIS

As explained in the first chapter, soon after we are
born, we develop a basic flaw—self-centeredness.
We think the world revolves around us and every-
one else is here to make us comfortable and happy. First, we get
all our needs taken care of, and then we start getting things from
these people. Then we start getting more things, and then we can't
seen to get enough. As we grow older we not only see all the things
other people have, but see and hear ads every day that tell us we
should have more—and that we deserve it. Gimmee, gimmee,
gimmee!

Then some of the harsh realities of life set in. Two of the first
lessons we learn are "NO," as in "you can't touch or have that," and
"SHARE," as in "you can't have it all to yourself." Talk about hard
lessons! So as we mature, we come to realize that we're really *not* the
center of the universe, even though we'd like to be. It also occurs to
us that the people we like and admire the most are the ones who
are caring, loving, and giving. Another thought that dawns on us is
that we'd much rather be around these kinds of people than around
uncaring, cold, and selfish people. And somewhere along the line

we're faced with an important question: Which kind of persons do *we* want to be—givers or takers? Our minds, because of what goes into them every day, often tell us to be takers, and to get all we can. But our hearts and our consciences tell us that it's really better to be givers. And the battle rages on for a lifetime. It comes with the territory of being human.

I'm not implying here that we shouldn't want "nice things," as in homes, cars, clothes, bank accounts, and the various toys we enjoy. There's nothing wrong with either wanting or having them. Many people have worked hard and made sacrifices to get to a comfortable place in life and to have some of those "things" that were beyond their reach when they were younger and struggling to make ends meet. As they see others going through that same struggle now, they're reminded that they've paid their dues. They finally earned a piece of the American Dream—and rightfully believe that they deserve it.

Earning a good life for ourselves, and having the money and things that come with it, is not the problem. The problem is when that money and those things become too important. Then they start owning us. When they do, we start suffering from a universal disease called "more." We can never answer the question, "How much is enough?" I've known a number of people, as I'm sure you have, who worked hard to earn a good living, but always had to have more. While trying to get more they ruined their lives and damaged the lives of others as well. We read and hear about these kinds of people almost every day. It's what happens when we don't understand that giving and receiving, reaping and sowing, are part of the natural flow of life.

You have to sow before you can reap. You have to give before you can get.

—ROBERT COLLIER

We make a living by what we get; we make a life by
what we give.

—WINSTON CHURCHILL

When I was growing up there were two famous comedians who were known as much for their giving as for their entertaining. Both were wildly popular and won awards for their work on TV and in the movies. But their charitable work was far more important to them. They were, and still are, perfect examples of being a blessing to others. Their names are Danny Thomas and Bob Hope.

Thomas, who lived from 1914 to 1991, was the father of Marlo Thomas, the actress and author, and is best remembered for the TV programs *Make Room for Daddy* and *The Danny Thomas Show,* two of the more popular family programs of his era. But Thomas's real passion, after his faith and his family, was St. Jude Children's Research Hospital, which he founded in Memphis in 1962. He donated much of his fortune and devoted the last thirty years of his life to helping sick children. He won countless humanitarian awards, including the Congressional Medal of Honor. He believed that real success was in the giving, not the getting:

Success in life has nothing to do with what you gain in life or
accomplish for yourself. It's what you do for others.

—DANNY THOMAS

Hope, who lived from 1903 to 2003, was one of the most beloved and enduring comedians of all time. His movies, TV specials, and jokes endeared him to millions of fans, popes, and presidents. Like Thomas, he is also remembered as much for what he gave as for how he made us laugh. He and his wife Dolores gave millions of dollars to Catholic Charities, and Hope toured the world for almost sixty years just to entertain our troops at

Christmastime. It started in 1941 during World War II, and continued through the Korean and Vietnam wars. When there were no wars going on, he found troops that were stationed in far parts of the globe, and he went to entertain them. He was honored by Congress five times because he had a heart for others and for charity.

> *If you haven't got any charity in your heart, you have the worst kind of heart problem.*
>
> —BOB HOPE

FOUR TYPES OF GIVING

1. Things

> *One man's junk is another man's treasure.*
>
> —WISE OLD SAYING

This is the easiest of the four types of giving. In fact, it's a stretch to even call it giving. It usually doesn't require us to make a sacrifice, but it can be of great benefit to others. Clothing and furniture are the most common things to give, but also appreciated by others are food, tools, toys, and even cars. Most of the time we're really just clearing out closets or rooms of unneeded things, but they can be of great value to people who have little. There are hundreds of charitable organizations that will not only be happy to accept our unwanted goods, They will often come and pick them up.

Do yourselves and others a favor. Unclutter your homes and clean out your closets regularly. There are people out there who would treasure some of your junk.

2. Blood

Do something amazing today. Save a life. Give blood.
—NATIONAL BLOOD SERVICE

Several years ago one of my best friends was told by his doctor that he would need heart bypass surgery if he wanted to stick around for a while. He was also told that a lot of blood would be needed, and that he should ask friends and family to donate to a blood center in his name. When he asked me to donate, something I had never done before, my first thought was, "I don't like blood and I dislike needles even more." But this was a dear friend, and I knew he wouldn't hesitate if I asked him to do the same thing. So I gave blood.

It turned out to be a far less painful experience than I had expected. I didn't watch the needle go in or watch the blood come out. I relaxed in a comfortable lounger in the company of a lot of nice people, enjoyed the moment, and was even rewarded with some cookies and juice when it was all over. The best part was the good feeling I had while leaving. It was that feeling that always comes when we do something for someone else. It also increased my awareness of just how much blood is needed daily, so I signed up to become a regular. I share this story, not to make myself look like a hero, but to encourage you to consider giving blood regularly.

3. Money

Money is like manure; it's not worth a thing unless it's spread around encouraging young things to grow.
—THORNTON WILDER

Giving away money is more difficult than giving away things we don't want any longer. Few people have money that they no longer want. Even the old money is still good. Giving away money is more difficult than giving blood because the money won't automatically replenish itself like blood does. Giving away things and giving away blood don't cost a cent. Giving away money can be downright expensive.

People with great wealth have little difficulty in giving away large sums of money for one simple reason: They have more than they could ever spend in several lifetimes. I don't mean to belittle this type of contribution. These people give voluntarily, and society benefits in many ways. I'm simple saying that it's easier to give when you have more than you need. The great industrialist Andrew Carnegie called surplus wealth a "sacred trust," and suggested that those who possess it have a moral obligation to use it for the good of the community. Most people would agree with him. What most people might *not* agree on is when money qualifies as "surplus wealth." It's a problem most of us will never have—even though we'd like to give it a try.

The truth is that money is an absolute necessity. When we have barely enough to meet our most basic needs (I was there for several years), it's difficult to give even some of it away. But it *is* still possible, and the best part is that only good will come from it. I promise. There really is a natural law of giving. As the quote by Wynn Davis at the beginning of this chapter states, "The law works to give us back more than we have sown." There will always be someone who needs money more than we do, and we have a moral responsibility to help when we can. I'm not suggesting that we be foolish and give our money away indiscriminately, but that we look for opportunities to help someone with less. It always benefits both the receiver and the giver.

There's no set formula for giving, and I will not suggest one. The concept of tithing has been handed down since the writing of the Old Testament. It means giving ten percent, usually to your place of worship. Some churches require it, some don't. Some people practice it rigorously, while others give more or less than ten percent based on the dictates of their conscience. Whatever the rule or the reason, real giving comes from the heart.

4. Yourself

You give but little when you give of your possessions. It is when you give of yourself that you truly give.

—KAHLIL GIBRAN

Now comes the hard part. It's easy to understand what it means to give things, blood, or money to other people, and we're just as clear on how to give them. But giving of *ourselves* isn't quite so specific. What does it mean, and how do we go about it? Giving of ourselves means doing something that helps other people. It can be physical, emotional, social, or spiritual help. This kind of help is purely altruistic, has no self-serving motives, and expects nothing in return. It comes only from the goodness in our hearts. We give of ourselves because we know what a blessing it is to be helped by others. We give of ourselves because people are in need. We give of ourselves because we're dependent upon one another. And we give of ourselves because it makes us feel more fully human.

WHAT CAN WE GIVE?
15 SPECIAL GIFTS THAT HARDLY COST A CENT

Perhaps above all else it is the gift of our time—the most perishable commodity we have—that means the most.

—THE EDEN PROJECT

It's been said often that "love" is a four-letter word, and it's spelled T-I-M-E. Alan Lakein, an expert on using time efficiently, says, "Time is life." So, we could also say that "love" is a four-letter word, and it's spelled L-I-F-E. There's no greater gift anyone can give than a piece of his or her life. If time is life and one's life is a gift to others, then it would follow that there's a third way to spell the word "love"—it's a four-letter word spelled G-I-V-E. When we give our time we give our lives. It's the foundation of these fifteen special gifts. You may not have previously thought of them as gifts, but they are. If you look upon them in this way you'll be much more likely give them and be a blessing to others.

1. THE GIFT OF PERSONAL COMMUNICATION. How do you feel when someone contacts you out of the blue for the sole purpose of reminding you that you're a treasured friend? You feel the same way everyone else does—special, loved, appreciated. And you can brighten someone else's life any day of the week. This can be done with a phone call, a handwritten note, or an e-mail, and none take more than a few minutes.

2. THE GIFT OF QUOTATIONS. I've never met anyone who doesn't appreciate a good quotation. That's why I put so many of them in my books—they're a gift to my readers, especially those who have expressed appreciation for them. The beauty of a good quotation is that it's brief, to the point, full of wisdom and advice, and a boost for the spirit. Find them, collect them, and share them. It's a simple way of giving someone a lift.

3. THE GIFT OF A GOOD RECOMMENDATION. When you make a great discovery, one that in some way enriches your life, share it with others. It could be a book (like this one, I hope), a play, a movie, a restaurant, a recipe, an article, a product, a service, a TV program, or a music CD. When you make these kinds of recommendations, you're really saying, "This brought some joy to my life. I want it to do the same for you."

4. THE GIFT OF A HELPING HAND.   All of us appreciate it when someone not only *offers* to help, but actually follows through. We're all faced with tasks—some big, some small; some important, some trivial; some requiring skill, some menial. Whatever it is, it always goes better with the help of another person. Whether on the job, at home, in school, or out socially, the gift of help is always appreciated.

5. THE GIFT OF LAUGHTER.   I've never met anyone who didn't like to laugh. It's one of the happiest and most healthy activities known to the human race. Victor Borge said, "Laughter is the shortest distance between two people." It's also a life enhancer and a great gift, one that can be given easily and often. Don't let those funny jokes, stories, bloopers, signs, and one-liners fade away. Share them with others.

6. THE GIFT OF LISTENING.   There are many times when someone close to us wants only one thing—our full and undivided attention. Listening intently to another person, with our eyes and with our hearts, silently says, "What you have to say, and the feelings behind your words, are important. Right now this is the best gift I can give you. I value our friendship."

7. THE GIFT OF AN INVITATION.   I regard all invitations, whether to a major event, a wedding, a party, a sporting event, or lunch with a friend, as special gifts. Whenever we ask someone to join us, we're really saying, "I want you to be there. Your company is cherished. You have something good to offer." We all want to be included, to be asked to join in, for a simple reason—sharing experiences with other people is one of the greatest joys of life.

8. THE GIFT OF PHYSICAL AFFECTION.   How do you feel when someone gives you a hug, a warm handshake, a friendly pat on the back, a kiss on the cheek, an affectionate touch? If you're a normal, red-blooded, breathing, living human being, you feel great. Alan Loy McGinnis, an esteemed counselor and author, advises, "Use your body to demonstrate warmth." With the right people and in the proper setting, that's exactly what acts of fondness do. Give this gift of affection liberally.

9. THE GIFT OF APPRECIATION.   When someone does something thoughtful for us, regardless of its nature, it's a gift. We can give another gift in return simply by expressing our appreciation. The great psychologist and philosopher William James said, "The deepest principle in human nature is the craving to be appreciated." We can satisfy that craving, and give a gift, every time we express our appreciation.

10. THE GIFT OF GOOD ADVICE.   Not everyone asks for it or wants it, but there are times when good advice is the greatest gift of all. The reason is that it can change lives. Countless accomplished people throughout history have cited good advice as the key to their success. When the opportunity is there and the other person is willing to listen, never hesitate to give this precious gift.

11. THE GIFT OF ENCOURAGEMENT.   One of the greatest things you can do for another person is give encouragement. The word means, literally, to give courage. Sometimes it's all a person needs to get started on something important. History is full of stories about people who achieved great things because of someone else's encouragement.

> *Flatter me, and I may not believe you.*
> *Criticize me, and I may not like you.*
> *Ignore me, and I may not forgive you.*
> *Encourage me, and I may not forget you.*
>
> —William Arthur

12. The gift of patience.   This is actually a dual gift, because patience always comes as the result of understanding. That's what we most want from other people, especially those closest to us. We especially need their patience and understanding when we're not at our best. They're gifts that enrich relationships by allowing them to grow. We can give the same gift to our family members, friends, and colleagues.

13. The gift of empathy.   Any time we can share feelings with another person, whether they're of sorrow or joy, we give a treasured gift. When Cathy's dad died unexpectedly in his mid-fifties some years ago, she experienced both shock and loss. The greatest comfort she received was from people who had also lost a parent under similar circumstances. They were able to identify with her, understand what she was going through, offer hope, and let her know they were there for her.

14. The gift of forgiveness.   This is the ultimate win-win gift. Both the giver and the receiver get something of great value—healing. We're all in need of it because we've all been hurt and offended by someone else. It makes it easier to forgive them when we remind ourselves that we've also caused pain in others.

Forgiveness releases us from unnecessary negative emotions and allows us to move on to better things.

15. THE GIFT OF PRAYER. It was not a coincidence that I received an e-mail, a phone call, and a handwritten note about prayer while writing this chapter. Each one was from a dear friend who was not only thinking about me but praying for me. What made the gift even more special was that I hadn't asked for the prayers. Since I look upon prayer—communication with God—as the highest activity of which a human being is capable, and because I know the sincerity of these people, their gifts became lasting treasures.

TWO EXPERTS ON THE SPIRIT OF GIVING

Albert Schweitzer: "Have reverence for life"

Mother Teresa: "Do ordinary things with extraordinary love"

The most important thing about genuine giving is the spirit in which it's done. Two of the greatest givers of all time left us with some wonderful advice about *how* to give. One was Albert Schweitzer (1875–1965), the musician, Protestant theologian, and medical missionary in Africa. The other was Mother Teresa (1910–1997), the Catholic nun and missionary to the poor and dying in India. These are two great Nobel Peace Prize winners who spent most of their joy-filled lives giving to others. Because I can't match either their giving or their eloquence, I'll let them explain the spirit of giving in their own words:

Albert Schweitzer

Until he extends his circle of compassion to include all living things, man will not find peace himself.

I don't know what your destiny will be, but one thing I do know: The only ones among you who will be really happy are those who have sought and found how to serve.

You must give some of your time to your fellow men.

Even if it's a little thing, do something for others—something for which you get no pay but the privilege of doing it.

Constant kindness can accomplish much. As the sun makes ice melt, kindness causes misunderstanding, mistrust, and hostility to evaporate.

Mother Teresa

It's not how much we give but how much love we put into giving.

Always have a cheerful smile. Don't only give your care, but give your heart as well.

There is a terrible hunger for love. We all experience that in our lives—the pain, the loneliness. We must have the courage to recognize it. The poor you may have in your own family. Find them. Love them.

Good works are links that form a chain of love.

We are all pencils in the hand of God.

EIGHT MORE EXPERTS ON THE JOY OF GIVING

Here, in the words of some of the wisest people ever to grace the earth, are a few of the best reasons to give:

For in giving freely without guarantee of return, you set into motion an irresistible momentum of goodness.
When we give, everyone is a winner.

—JOHN MARKS TEMPLETON

There is no happiness in having or in getting, but only in giving.

—HENRY DRUMMOND

Every charitable act is a stepping stone towards heaven.

—HENRY WARD BEECHER

For it is in giving that we receive.

—ST. FRANCIS OF ASSISI

I have found that among its other benefits, giving liberates the soul of the giver.

—MAYA ANGELOU

He who obtains has little. He who scatters has much.

—LAO-TZU

It is one of the most beautiful compensations of life that no man can sincerely try to help another without helping himself.

—RALPH WALDO EMERSON

Giving brings happiness at every stage of its expression. We
experience joy in forming the intention to be generous. We
experience joy in the actual act of giving something. We
experience joy in remembering the fact that
we have given.

—BUDDHA

There's one more reason to give. In his classic book *The Art of Loving,* Erich Fromm says that when we give we get a "heightened vitality" of what it means to be human. What do we give to others? Fromm says we give others all that is alive in us—our interest, our understanding, our knowledge, our humor, everything in us that's good. In doing so, we enhance the sense of aliveness in others while enhancing our own. Through the act of genuine and selfless giving we experience life at a deeper level and come to know the real meaning of joy.

It is more blessed to give than to receive.

—ACTS 20:35

Chapter Five

FORGIVENESS

LEARN TO FORGIVE. IT'S INCREDIBLY
HARD, BUT WORTH THE EFFORT—
AND ESSENTIAL TO MENTAL HEALTH.

DEFINITIONS

*Forgive: to cease to feel resentment against (an offender);
allowing room for error or weakness.*

—MERRIAM-WEBSTER

*It is the foregoing of resentment or revenge when the
wrongdoer's actions deserve it and giving the gifts of mercy,
generosity, and love when the wrongdoer does not deserve
them.*

—INTERNATIONAL FORGIVENESS INSTITUTE

RELATED WORDS/ VIRTUES

Mercy
Healing
Reconciliation

OPPOSITE WORDS/ FLAWS

Resentment
Revenge
Bitterness

5. Forgiveness

LIFE'S BIGGEST CHALLENGE?

Forgiveness is a basic, daily challenge. It comes in big sizes and small. The challenge of forgiveness has been with us from the beginning of human consciousness.

—ROGER BERTSCHAUSEN

Life is an adventure in forgiveness.

—NORMAN COUSINS

For many readers, this might be the most challenging chapter in the book—not to read, but to practice. For the author, this might be the most challenging chapter in the book—not to write, but to practice. The truth is, everyone struggles with forgiveness. Some understand the benefits of it, work at it, and master it. Others try, but just can't seem to let go of their hurts, and continue to suffer. Regardless of the person, the circumstances, or the degree of pain involved, forgiveness is a challenge. It's not something that comes naturally to us. It's one of the most difficult of all virtues to acquire.

Several years ago I was getting some counseling and reading a book about forgiveness for the simple reason that I was full of anger toward a person who had betrayed me and hurt me deeply. Intellectually, I knew this anger was unhealthy and was preventing me from living peacefully. But emotionally, I couldn't seem to let go. As I shared my battle with some close friends, they all made one similar comment—it was their belief that every person struggles with forgiveness. At this same time I shared with the high-school seniors in my psychology class that I was reading a book about the healing power of forgiveness. I asked them, "How many of you have ever struggled with forgiveness?" Every right hand in the class went up immediately. And although I didn't ask for any comments, I got plenty. I remember two distinctly: "It's *impossible* to forgive," and, "I know someone whom I'll *never* forgive, and don't ever want to."

A few nights later I asked my university students, all adults in their thirties and forties, if they had a hard time with forgiveness. The response was the same—everyone did. And once again, I heard the "impossible" and "never" comments. Shortly afterward, I posed the same question to a group of teachers I was speaking to at a conference. Same results. Even in churches, where forgiveness is preached often, not only as a virtue, but as a directive from God, people of strong faith readily admit that it's one of their biggest challenges. And just after you work hard, win the battle, and forgive someone who's hurt you, someone else comes along and nails you. Forgiveness is, indeed, a daily challenge. If you struggle with it, you're not alone.

One of the things that points out just how difficult it is to forgive, and what a universal struggle it is, is the sheer amount of material that has been written on the subject. In my research for this chapter I found no fewer than twenty-two books and countless articles and essays written about it. Most of the authors approach forgiveness from a religious viewpoint. They see forgiveness as a spiritual process, and use these two well-known passages from Scripture as their foundation:

> *If you forgive other people their failures, your Heavenly Father*
> *will also forgive you. But if you will not forgive, . . . neither*
> *will your Heavenly Father forgive you your failures.*
>
> —MATTHEW 6:14–15

*Then Peter approached him with the question, "Master, how
many times can my brother wrong me and I must forgive him?
Would seven times be enough?" "No," replied Jesus, "not seven
times, but seventy times seven!"*

—MATTHEW 18:21–22

People in fields related to counseling have written most of the
other books, and their approach to forgiveness is purely psychological. Their emphasis is on the damage we do to ourselves when
we refuse to forgive, and on the mental health rewards of learning
to forgive. While all the books I looked at offered valuable advice,
two of them stood out. They are *The Art of Forgiving: When You
Need to Forgive and Don't Know How,* by Lewis B. Smedes, and
Forgive for Good: A Proven Prescription for Health and Happiness, by
Dr. Fred Luskin. Smedes has written two books on forgiveness, the
first one in 1984, and this one in 1997. He taught ethics and the-
ology for many years at Fuller Theological Seminary in Pasadena,
California. His approach is both spiritual and psychological.
Luskin is the director and co-founder of the Stanford University
Forgiveness Project. His book came out in 2002, made several best-
seller lists, and is based on the most recent psychological research
in the field of forgiveness. Both books are easy to read and full of
practical advice. I highly recommend them, particularly if you
want to learn more about the benefits of forgiveness. There's a limit
to what I can cover in a single chapter, but I will try to summarize
some of the main points of these experts.

FACTS ABOUT FORGIVENESS—
WHAT IT IS AND WHAT IT ISN'T

Forgiveness is a process, not an event.

—ROSE SWEET

One of the main reasons so many people never experience the peace that comes with forgiving is that they don't fully understand what it is. Many of the false notions of what forgiveness is prevent them from even trying. Here are a few of the things that forgiveness is *not*. They may clear up some of the most common misconceptions about it:

- Forgiveness does not mean that you are condoning the hurtful behavior of another person, nor does it mean that you're letting that person off the hook.
- Forgiveness does not mean that you have to play the part of a martyr. It does not mean that you have to continue as a victim.
- Forgiveness does not mean that you have to pretend that everything is fine. Pain is real and forgiveness takes time.
- Forgiveness does not mean reconciliation. Many times it leads to restoring relationships, but it isn't always possible.
- Forgiveness does not mean forgetting. We're urged to "forgive and forget," but it isn't really possible to completely erase our memory banks. We can't deny reality, but we *can* forgive without forgetting.
- Forgiveness does not mean being a weakling. Forgiving a person who's hurt you is not "wimping out" on yourself; it's taking a step toward healing.

It also helps to understand what forgiveness *is*. It has several components, and as we come to recognize them, we become more likely to find the strength within us to become forgiving.

- Forgiveness is an attitude, which Merriam-Webster defines as "a mental position." It's a mindset that determines whether the hurt will continue or the healing will begin.

- Forgiveness is a choice. Since all attitudes are choices, we're always free to choose the methods by which we can best deal with our pain.
- Forgiveness is a process. It's not something we do the "quick and easy" way. It takes time and it takes hard work.
- Forgiveness is letting go of the past. This is the hardest, yet the most important part of the process. We can't enjoy the present when we're stuck in the past.
- Forgiveness is a form of healing. It's the only thing that allows us to move on after being hurt. It's realizing that we have better ways to spend our energy.
- Forgiveness is a sign of strength. Some people proudly claim to "never forgive," as if it's a trait to be admired. It isn't—it's a sign of weakness. Real forgiveness requires character and courage.

> *The weak can never forgive. Forgiveness is the attribute of the strong.*
>
> —MAHATMA GANDHI

THE COST OF RESENTMENT

> *Anytime you're filled with resentment, you're turning the controls of your emotional life over to others to manipulate.*
>
> —WAYNE DYER

> *Anger will never disappear as long as thoughts of resentment are cherished in the mind. Anger will disappear just as soon as thoughts of resentment are forgotten.*
>
> —BUDDHA

Here are five simple questions for you:

1. Would you deliberately poison yourself?
2. Would you voluntarily check yourself into prison even though you had done nothing wrong?
3. Would you load up two suitcases full of bricks and carry them around all day, even though they weight you down, yet serve no useful purpose?
4. Would you tie yourself to a torture rack and ask someone to inflict pain upon you?
5. Would you ask someone who's hurt you to hurt you some more, and to continue hurting you over and over?

These may seem to be silly questions, real no-brainers. Obviously, the answer to all of them is no. To do these things would be illogical, masochistic, and stupid. What normal person would choose to be hurt in these ways? Yet, that's exactly what we do when we refuse to forgive, or don't learn to forgive. We bring more hurt upon ourselves. Resentment poisons our minds, imprisons us, weighs us down, and allows someone to inflict pain upon us. And the truth is, if we're allowing this to happen, then we are, indeed, asking someone to continue to hurt us. This is the real cost of resentment—we're actually choosing to suffer.

> *I believe that to withhold forgiveness is to choose to continue to remain the victim. Remember, you always have the choice.*
> —LARRY JAMES

The most important thing to understand about resentment, or lack of forgiveness, is that you're allowing the pain to continue.

You're giving the person who hurt you an extension of negative power over your feelings. Yet you don't have to. That other person who has you steamed is probably out having a good time right now, and not even thinking about you. Why should you be thinking about him or her? Aren't there better things to occupy your mind?

FORGIVENESS CAN BE LEARNED

Forgiveness is a trainable skill just like learning to throw a baseball.

—Dr. Fred Luskin

If we really want to love, we must learn how to forgive.

—Mother Teresa

No matter how impossible it may seem under some circumstances, forgiveness *can* be learned. As indicated at the beginning of this chapter, it's an ongoing challenge, it's hard to do, and it's hard to sustain. But it's worth the effort and energy it takes because genuine forgiveness continually produces positive results. It may or may not lead to reconciliation, but it always leads to healing and peace of mind. Those are great reasons to learn to forgive.

The starting place for forgiveness is reminding ourselves that, because we're human, and because we have feelings, we're going to get hurt from time to time. Everybody does. We also need to remind ourselves that we've hurt others from time to time. Everybody does that, too. Pain happens. There's a simple reason why it happens: We're flawed, as in self-centered, and we sometimes do insensitive and hurtful things to one another. Since pain is part of life, we live more effectively when we learn how to manage it, whether it's physical or emotional. It's necessary, not only for survival, but for growth. It's also a skill in which we make an important choice:

Pain is inevitable. Misery is optional.

—TIM HANSEL

Once we've accepted these realities of life, it helps to learn some specific strategies for dealing with our hurts. For lack of a better name, one I've used and taught for years is called "Flip the switch." It came from three major points that I made regularly and emphatically during my many years as a psychology teacher:

1. Attitude is the starting place for everything we do.
2. We're always free to choose an attitude that works for us or against us.
3. A good attitude beats a bad attitude every time.

Many of my students told me that they clearly understood these concepts intellectually, but that it was much more difficult to apply them to everyday living. A surprising number of them admitted that negative thinking was a real problem. The two most common questions were "How do you stop negative thoughts from coming into your head?" and, "How do you deal with negative thoughts if they just keep popping up?" The answer to the first question was, "No one can entirely stop them from coming. The more important thing is to learn how to deal with them." The answer to the second question was, "Flip the switch." This always evoked some blank stares and the ever-popular question, "Huh?" This was always interpreted correctly as "What do you mean?"

I asked my students to try to imagine a light switch inside each of their brains. Instead of saying "On" and "Off" it has an "N" in the down position and a "P" in the up position. They stand for "Negative" and "Positive." Ideally, we'd like to have the switch in the up, or P, position all the time. But for some unexplainable reason, it sometimes gets pushed to the down, or N position. When this happens things get dark, just like when the light switch gets turned off. So, in order to get out of the dark, we do a simple thing—we flip the switch.

In other words, as soon as we realize that negative thoughts have crept in and are dragging us down, we change them. We always have that choice because we have control of the switch. Since resentment is negative, and forgiveness is positive, it's healthier to move the switch back to the P position each time we realize that it's somehow slipped down to N. Several of my students thought it was a good idea to have two switches because they saw forgiveness as a separate issue from just positive and negative thinking.

One woman, who had recently gone through a painful divorce and was struggling with forgiveness, said she had a double switch plate in her head. One was P and N, the other was F and R, for forgiveness and resentment. She said that whenever her switch was in the R position, she realized that the other switch was in the N position. Because it was a double plate, she could flip both switches up at the same time. She said, "It may sound silly, but this simple concept has really helped me move on. That set of switches reminds me that I always have choices about what's going to occupy my mind."

In his wonderful book *Forgive for Good*, Dr. Luskin suggests a similar, but more specific idea. He calls it "Changing the channel on your remote control." Instead of a light switch in our imaginations, we have a remote control that allows us to change the program. Instead of watching the anger and resentment channel, we can watch something more pleasant. He even mentions four specific channels that always have something good on: the Gratitude Channel, the Beauty Channel, the Forgiveness Channel, and the Love Channel. He also gives several examples of the great programming we can see on each one. The most important thing to remember is that we have total control over the channel changer. It helps us learn to forgive.

> *Life may not be perfect, but you can learn to suffer less. You can learn to forgive, and you can learn to heal.*
>
> —DR. FRED LUSKIN

A TOP-TEN LIST OF THE BENEFITS OF FORGIVENESS

> *Forgiveness is almost a selfish act because of its immense benefits to the one who forgives.*
>
> —LAWANA BLACKWELL

> *Forgiveness is a gift that you give to yourself.*
>
> —LARRY JAMES

1. Forgiveness brings an end to self-defeating behavior.

> *You practice forgiveness for two reasons. One is to let others know that you no longer wish to be in a state of hostility with that person; and two, to free yourself from the self-defeating energy of resentment.*
>
> —WAYNE DYER

Forgiveness breaks the self-defeating cycle of anger and resentment, which only hold us back. We learn to forgive so we can overcome these demons, experience the emotional relief, and move on with our lives.

—SARAH BUCKLEY, M.D.

2. Forgiveness moves us out of the past.

Not to forgive is to be imprisoned by the past, by grievances that do not permit life to proceed with new business.

—ROBIN CASARJIAN

Forgiveness means letting go of the past.

—GERALD JAMPOLSKY

3. Forgiveness sets us free and allows us to move on.

To forgive is to set a prisoner free and discover that the prisoner was you.

—LEWIS B. SMEDES

When you hold resentment toward another, you are bound to that person or condition by an emotional link that is stronger than steel. Forgiveness is the only way to dissolve that link and get free.

—CATHERINE PONDER

4. Forgiveness makes us better persons.

Keeping score of old scores and scars, getting even and one-upping, always makes you less than you are.

—MALCOLM FORBES

Doing an injury puts you below your enemy; Revenging one makes you but even with him; Forgiving it sets you above him.
—BENJAMIN FRANKLIN

5. Forgiveness strengthens our character.

Never does the human soul appear so strong as when it forgoes revenge, and dares to forgive an injury.
—E. H. CHAPIN

Strength of character means the ability to overcome resentment against others, to hide hurt feelings, and to forgive quickly.
—LAWRENCE G. LOVASIK

6. Forgiveness makes us more loving.

We cannot love unless we have accepted forgiveness, and the deeper our experience of forgiveness is, the greater is our love.
—PAUL TILLICH

Forgiveness is the final form of love.
—REINHOLD NIEBUHR

7. Forgiveness improves our mental and physical health.

Scientific research clearly shows that learning to forgive is good for one's health and well-being, good for mental health, and according to recent data, good for physical health as well.
—DR. FRED LUSKIN

People who replace anger, hostility, and hatred with forgiveness will have better cardiovascular health and fewer long-term health problems.
—CARL THORESEN, PH.D.

8. Forgiveness gives us peace of mind.

Forgiving those who hurt us is the key to personal peace.

—G. WEATHERLY

Forgiveness is an inner correction that lightens the heart. It is for our peace of mind first. Being at peace, we will now have peace to give others, and this is the most permanent and valuable gift we can possibly give.

—GERALD JAMPOLSKY

9. Forgiveness increases our wisdom.

Forgiveness is an essential part of wisdom.

—ERWIN G. HALL

A wise man will make haste to forgive, because he knows the true value of time, and will not suffer it to pass away in unnecessary pain.

—SAMUEL JOHNSON

10. Forgiveness honors God.

It is in pardoning that we are pardoned.

—ST. FRANCIS OF ASSISI

Pardon, not wrath, is God's best attribute.

—BAYARD TAYLOR

Be kind to each other, tenderhearted, forgiving one another, just as God has forgiven you.

—EPHESIANS 4:32

Chapter Six

THINKING

THE MIND IS LIKE A GARDEN. FEED IT AND WEED IT WITH CARE.

DEFINITIONS

Think: To form or have in the mind. Think implies the entrance of an idea into one's mind.

—MERRIAM-WEBSTER

Thinking: a psychological function that involves the creation and organization of information in the mind.

—THOMSON, *LEARNING: PATHWAYS TO PSYCHOLOGY*

RELATED WORDS/ VIRTUES	OPPOSITE WORDS/ FLAWS
Understanding	Ignorant
Open-minded	Close-minded
Aware	Unaware

6. Thinking

I think, therefore I am.

—RENÉ DESCARTES

A mind is a terrible thing to waste.

—UNITED NEGRO COLLEGE FUND

As mentioned in the Introduction, I first learned about the concept of free will from the Jesuits at the University of San Francisco. It was at the heart of their teaching system, which included heavy emphasis on philosophy and logic—in other words, THINKING! I still recall vividly the first words we heard at freshmen orientation. The dean of students said: "You're here to get an education. But before we can give it to you, we first have to teach you to think." I had no idea what he meant. I thought we had learned to think a long time ago, around the time we learned to talk. And I was sure that we had done a lot of thinking while working our way through high school. What did he mean by teaching us to think?

We found out what he meant on the first day of classes. One of the courses we were all required to take was Logic. Father Vaughn, the professor, started by asking us if we remembered what the dean of students had said a few days earlier about "teaching us to think." We did. He said, "Well, this is where it all begins." What we learned was that there were higher levels of thinking than the ones we had previously been exposed to, and that's why we were in college. It started with Logic, and continued through a series of required philosophy courses for eight consecutive semesters. These courses were challenging, enlightening, sometimes confusing, occasionally boring, frequently entertaining, and always valuable. We did, indeed, learn to think.

One of the questions that Father Vaughn asked us on that first day in Logic was: "What is it that separates humans from animals?" After much discussion, we learned that the two main answers were language and higher-order thinking skills. Humans can speak to each other articulately, and among their thinking processes they can imagine, reason, deduce, speculate, solve problems, and make predictions. Once these basic concepts had been established, Father Vaughn made another point about thinking that none of us ever forgot. It began with another question: "What is the most important part in each of your bodies?" We suggested that it was the brain, and he agreed.

Father Vaughn called it the "control center" for everything we think and do. He said the problem was that most people never learn to operate it as effectively as they could, and that this usually results in unfulfilled lives. He said it wasn't a matter of high or low IQ. It was a matter of making the most of the intelligence we were given. He said history is full of stories about people with ordinary intelligence who've done extraordinary things with their lives. And there have always been people of superior intellect and/or talent who've done little or nothing with their lives. The difference, he said, is in how people think: "Our thoughts rule our lives."

> *The things you think about determine the quality of your life.*
> *Your soul takes on the color of your thoughts.*
> —MARCUS AURELIUS

ARE THE BRAIN AND THE MIND THE SAME?

S ince the terms "brain" and "mind" were both used in this first class, several students wanted to know if they were the same. The answer was no, although many people use them interchangeably. Here's how Merriam-Webster differentiates the two:

Brain: "The portion of the vertebrate central nervous system that constitutes the organ of thought and neural coordination . . . ; intellectual endowment."
Mind: "The element or complex of elements in an individual that feels, perceives, thinks, wills, and especially reasons."

Another way of distinguishing between the two is this:

Brain: The physical organ inside a person's head that operates as his or her control center. It's similar to the hard drive on a computer. It's the vessel in which the electronic impulses that create thought are contained.
Mind: The content stored in the brain, as in thoughts, feelings, and memories. It's similar to the software in our computers. The mind is what's inside the hard drive; it's the ability to control what we think and what we do.

> *It is not the brains that matter most, but that which guides them—*
> *the character, the heart, generous qualities, progressive ideas.*
> —FYODOR DOSTOYEVSKY

After distinguishing between the brain and the mind, Father Vaughn suggested we needed to learn two important things regarding the thought process. The first was what he called the "care and feeding" of the mind. The second was to learn how to operate this vital control center at maximum efficiency. He said it didn't require a college education to learn to perform either of these important functions. He said, "You can learn everything you need to know about successful operation of the brain from good mentors and good books." Then he reemphasized the point that many people don't succeed in life because they don't learn either how to nurture their minds or how to operate them effectively. These are the main two points in this chapter.

CARE AND FEEDING OF THE MIND

The care and feeding of the mind is just as important as the care and feeding of the body. The mind unfed weakens just as the body does. The mind not sustained by the continual intake of something that is capable of filling it well or nourishing it, shrinks and shrivels.

—MORTIMER ADLER

The process of *caring* for mind begins with *opening* it. This is another one of those first-day-of-college lessons that I'll never forget. Dr. Brusher, my professor in the first of those eight required philosophy courses, wanted to discuss the purpose of an education with us before he introduced his subject. He said, "The purpose of an education is not to *fill* your mind—that's impossible anyway. The purpose of an education is to first *open* your mind, and then to expand it. The more you learn, the more you'll understand how little you know and how much more there is yet to learn. Hopefully, it will make you want to learn more. This is what keeps us sharp. And it all starts with an open mind."

There's a big difference between an empty head and an open mind. An open mind is really an attitude of receptiveness, being open to new information and to other points of view. It helps us becomes aware of our own limitations, it helps us develop more empathy and understanding, and it helps us think better.

> *An open mind is the beginning of self-discovery and growth. We can't learn anything new until we can admit that we don't already know everything.*
>
> —ERWIN G. HALL

Caring for the Mind

On the title page of this chapter it says, "The mind is like a garden. Feed it and weed it with care." This way of looking at the mind comes from a little book considered by many to be a classic. It was written in 1904 by James Allen, and is titled *As a Man Thinketh*. More than a hundred years later, many accomplished people not only give the book credit for their success, but claim they continue to read it at least once a year. Here's the heart of his message:

> *Just as the gardener cultivates his plot, keeping it free from weeds, and growing the flowers and fruits which he requires, so may a man tend the garden of his mind, weeding out all the wrong, useless, and impure thoughts, and cultivating toward perfection the flowers and fruits of right, useful, and pure thoughts.*
>
> —JAMES ALLEN

Allen's analogy is priceless. The mind is the garden, the weeds are negative and destructive thoughts, and the flowers and fruits are positive and constructive thoughts. It really hits home when you enjoy gardening as much as I do. I plant flowers every spring and fall, and take great pleasure in watching them bloom and grow more colorful and beautiful. But just planting them is not enough. They must be fed and they must be cared for, as in keeping the weeds out. Those pesky weeds appear in our gardens just like negative thoughts pop up in our minds—seemingly out of nowhere. And if they're not pulled out quickly and regularly, they take over and choke the life out of the flowers, destroying the garden. If they're cleaned out regularly, the flowers have room to grow and the garden stays healthy—just like the mind does.

Feeding the Mind

That garden also needs to be fed. It needs a fertile soil at the beginning, and then needs regular amounts of nourishment to stay healthy and grow. The fertile soil in this case is an open mind, one that *wants* to be fed. This nourishment comes in the form of healthy ideas going into our minds regularly. They can come from a wide variety of sources: people, books and other publications, television, movies, the Internet, community events, and so on.

> *You are what you are because of what goes into your mind.*
> —ZIG ZIGLAR

The above quote is not only one of my all-time favorites, but the one I used most often during my teaching career. On the first day of class, whether with my teenage students or my adult students, I wrote this quote on the board and asked a simple question: "What does this mean?" Virtually everyone interpreted it the same way I did—whatever information is dominant in a person's mind will determine the direction of that person's life. I asked them if we can control everything that goes into our minds. Because we're bombarded with information, especially advertising, from so many different sources, it's impossible to have total control over everything that goes into our minds. But my students agreed with me that we *do* have choices—we can choose to screen out a high percentage of the trash, and we can choose to replace it with healthier material.

One of the main problems is that few people have ever been taught the importance of a healthy mental diet. They've never even heard of the concept. If they don't know there *is* such a thing as a healthy mental diet, then it would be safe to conclude that they aren't maintaining one. The sources of healthy ideas that I mentioned above (people, books, and so on) can just as easily be the sources of *un*healthy ideas. Let's face it—we live in a free market economy, and mental junk food is as hot a seller as is physical junk food. I'm not saying that we should never indulge in a little junk food. Candy is fun, and so is watching a dumb sitcom on occasion. But a steady diet of these things without any nourishment would ruin us. We *do* have choices.

Every successful person I've ever known has a system for maintaining a healthy mental diet. They have a steady stream of positive, nurturing, and uplifting ideas and information going into their heads. They're constantly stimulated and challenged. They weed and feed their minds daily.

The mind grows by what it feeds on.

—J. G. HOLLAND

THINKING AND CHARACTER— "WE BECOME WHAT WE THINK ABOUT"

The lessons learned about thinking in those first few days of college, and in the remaining four years, were of unparalleled value. I've always been grateful for the professors who helped us understand the power of the mind and taught us how to think at a higher level. Those lessons became even more meaningful several years later when I began to understand more clearly the relationship between thinking and character. The type of person we become begins with our thoughts.

I believed it when I was told that a college education was only the beginning, and I left with a great love of history, philosophy, and reading. The more I read the writings of wise people throughout the ages, the more I understood the importance of nurturing my thoughts. Here are ten brilliant thinkers who have taught us that our thoughts lead to our character and then to our destiny:

> *As a man thinketh in his heart, so is he.*
> —SOLOMON, PROVERBS 23:7. KING JAMES VERSION

> *The art of thinking is the greatest art of all. . . . The thinker knows he is today where his thoughts have taken him and that he is building his future by the quality of the thoughts he thinks.*
> —WILFRED PETERSON

> *A man is what he thinks about all day long.*
> —RALPH WALDO EMERSON

> *Your life is what your thoughts make it.*
> —MARCUS AURELIUS

> *A man is literally what he thinks, his character being the complete sum of all his thoughts.*
> —JAMES ALLEN

> *Man's greatness lies in the power of thought.*
> —BLAISE PASCAL

Thought is great and swift and free, the light of the world, and
the chief glory of man.

—BERTRAND RUSSELL

Nurture your mind with great thoughts, for you will never go
any higher than you think.

—BENJAMIN DISRAELI

We are the masters of our fate, the captains of our souls, because
we have the power to control our thoughts.

—NAPOLEON HILL

We become what we think about. Our minds are the steering
mechanisms of our lives.

—EARL NIGHTINGALE

Earl Nightingale is the most modern of these ten great
thinkers. He died in 1989 and left a world of wisdom behind, most
of it about the relationship between thinking and success. His legacy started in 1956, when Columbia Records produced
Nightingale's essay called "The Strangest Secret." It became the
first spoken message ever to receive a Golden Record for selling
more than a million copies. Keep in mind that this was in the era
before cassette tapes and CDs. The only thing heard on this classic
recording was Nightingale's voice. It became so popular, it eventually led to the forming of the Nightingale-Conant Corporation, the
first company to produce educational and inspirational recordings.

Nightingale's "secret" consisted of the first six words in his
quote above: "We become what we think about." He said it's the
one truth that every wise person throughout history has agreed
upon. Nightingale also pointed out that most schools teach us how
to remember, but not how to think. Apparently, he didn't know

about the Jesuits. But he's correct in pointing out an important flaw in our educational system. It does not emphasize thinking skills. He suggested there should be a required course called "Thinking" at every grade level of school and throughout college. He called thinking "the highest function of which the human is capable," and advised us not to take it for granted.

DOES "POSITIVE THINKING" REALLY WORK?

> *Positive thinking won't let you do anything, but it will let you do everything better than negative thinking will.*
>
> —ZIG ZIGLAR

> *Positive anything is better than negative nothing.*
>
> —ELBERT HUBBARD

There are a lot of wild claims about what positive thinking can do for us. The subject has been examined in regard to physical health, healing, performance in school, athletic achievement, business success, mental health, spiritual beliefs, and probably every other phase of life. Some of the theories are based on scientific research and deep thought, and some of them are just total nonsense. I guess I'm not a "positive affirmation" kind of guy. I don't happen to believe that looking at yourself in the mirror while repeating the mantra "I am lovable and capable" or "I am someone special" does anything except make you look silly and feel like a fool.

Zig Ziglar and Elbert Hubbard, in the quotes above, get right to the heart of the matter. Whether positive thinking works or not isn't really what's most important. The main point is in understanding what negative thinking does to us. By negative thinking,

I mean carrying around destructive thoughts in our heads, ones that can only hurt us. It's the worst form of masochism. It means choosing to inflict pain on yourself. Absolutely nothing good can come from it. No one ever achieved anything with negative thoughts and a defeatist attitude. At least with positive thinking, you give yourself a chance to accomplish something.

Here's a simple example: A scared Little Leaguer goes up to bat against the biggest, baddest, hardest-throwing pitcher in the league. The whole time he's thinking, "I know I'm going to strike out." It's almost guaranteed that he will. Let's say that same kid goes up there thinking, "Hey, other guys have hit this pitcher. I'll relax, take my cuts, and see what happens." This doesn't guarantee that he'll get a hit, but it sure increases his chances. As Ziglar says, positive thinking "will let you do everything better than negative thinking will." This is an important distinction. That's why it's so important to understand that positive thinking can't even begin to work if the mind is full of negative thoughts. So I want to reinforce a point that was made both in the chapter on forgiveness and earlier in this chapter. We *must* have a method for clearing our minds of these destructive intruders that are part of life. In the previous chapter I mentioned my technique called "flip the switch." I also explained Dr. Fred Luskin's suggestion to "change the channel" and James Allen's plan for "pulling up the weeds." There are a variety of imaginative ways for cleaning the trash out of our minds.

I have a friend who tells me that he "fumigates" regularly. He calls negative thoughts "little varmints." Try to imagine him telling me this in his southern drawl: "I don't know how them little varmints get in there. There must be a hole in the screen or somethin'. But they're pesky little devils, and they prevent me from gettin' my work done and enjoying myself. So I just go in there every time they show up and fumigate the hell out of 'em. Then I can get on with the business of living."

If the weeds are gone, the garden can grow. If the program is bad, you can change the channel and find something better. If you're in the dark, you can flip the light switch on. If you get rid of the bugs, you can have some peace. Do whatever works so you have room for good, wholesome, constructive thoughts. There's a bookstore in San Francisco that many people love. It's called "A Clean, Well-Lighted Place for Books." What a wonderful name! Think of your mind as a clean, well-lighted place for ideas. The key is keeping it clean and well-lighted.

Work joyfully and peacefully, knowing that right thoughts and right efforts will inevitably bring about right results.

—JAMES ALLEN

Chapter Seven

POSSIBILITIES

ALWAYS THINK IN TERMS OF
WHAT'S POSSIBLE. IT'S HOW EVERY
ACHIEVEMENT BEGINS.

DEFINITIONS

Possibility: the condition or fact of being possible; one's utmost power, capacity, or ability.

Possible: being within the limits of ability, capacity, or realization.

—MERRIAM-WEBSTER

Something that can be done; capable of happening or existing; "anything is possible."

—WORDREFERENCE.COM

RELATED WORDS/ VIRTUES

Opportunity
Potential
Imagination

OPPOSITE WORDS/ FLAWS

Close-mindedness
Hopelessness
Lack of imagination

7. Possibilities

Look at things . . . as they can be.
                    —DAVID JOSEPH SCHWARTZ

The previous chapter about thinking focused on the care and feeding of the mind—putting nourishing information into it and learning how to eliminate the destructive thoughts that seem to pop up as part of everyday life. This chapter focuses on more specific ways in which we can develop habits of constructive thinking. I want to share with my readers some thought-provoking, and sometimes mind-changing, activities that I did with both my teenage and adult students for many years. They're based on what I called the "Fabulous Four." I found that giving nicknames to various concepts, activities, and principles helped students better remember them. Another technique I used was the posting of "visible reminders." The ideas I most wanted my students to remember were prominently displayed on the walls of the classroom so they would be reinforced daily.

During the first week of school I handed out a sheet of paper that had five words on it: education, learning, knowledge, wisdom, and thinking. I asked my students to write their own definition of each. We then discussed their various interpretations of these terms, and worked out a consensus definition of each. My goal was to help them understand that each word had a different meaning, but that they were related, particularly in my classroom. The most emphasis was placed on the word "thinking," and I taught all of the concepts covered in the previous chapter.

At the beginning of the second week of school I put up five signs in the front of the room. Each one was in a different bright color and had a single word on it. The words were in bold, capital black letters. This is what they saw:

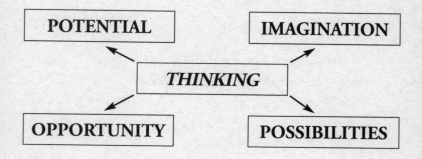

I introduced the signs by saying, "We've now advanced to thinking at its best. Welcome to the Fabulous Four." I asked them to take note that THINKING was in the middle, and that the other four were all connected to it. I then repeated four quotes I had used during the first week of school. These are the ones by Ralph Waldo Emerson, Marcus Aurelius, James Allen, and Blaise Pascal that are on pages 85–86. The central idea is: "We become what we think about."

Over the next two classes we did activities, followed by lengthy discussions, pertaining to each of the Fabulous Four. The purpose was to plant some seeds that would grow into patterns of constructive thinking. The feedback from these exercises was heartwarming. A high percentage of my students said that their awareness of the power of thoughts had been greatly increased, and that they had become far "better thinkers." A woman named Rose in one of my university classes said, "You know what I like most about all this thinking stuff? You don't try to teach us *what* to think; you teach us *how* to think." I loved it! I said, "My Jesuit professors would be proud."

NO. 1 OF THE FABULOUS FOUR: POTENTIAL

Compared to what we ought to be, we are only half awake.
We are making use of only a small part of our physical
and mental resources.

—William James

No matter what the level of your ability, you have more
potential than you can ever develop in a lifetime.

—James T. McKay

The activity.　I handed to each student a sheet of paper with word potential on the top. Below it were four questions, each with space to write in answers:

1. What is potential?
2. How much of his or her potential do you think the average person uses on a day-to-day basis?
3. How much of your potential do you think *you're* using on a day-to-day basis?
4. If your answer to number 3 is less than 100 percent, why aren't you using all of it?

The only thing my students agreed upon was the meaning of potential. It's what we're capable of, what we have the ability to do, what we *can* do. The answers to both questions 2 and 3 above ranged from 10 percent to 50 percent. Interesting, but not surprising, was the fact that most people saw themselves using far more of their potential than the average person. But rarely did I find a student who claimed to be operating at much higher than the 50 percent level. The most common answer to question 4 was, "Just lazy, I guess."

There is no one, neither the greatest psychologist nor the greatest mathematician, nor anyone else, who can give us precise figures on how much potential anyone is using at a given moment. But there is a well-accepted body of theory on this subject. Whether it comes from psychologist William James in the early 1900s, or from Albert Einstein in the latter 1900s, most people who have studied it claim that we habitually operate at less than 10 percent of our potential. Einstein himself said he was probably using less than 10 percent of his when he discovered the theory of relativity. The statement made by James at the top of this section is more than a hundred years old. Yet most experts would agree that it's no less true today. Most people operate well below their potential.

There's good news in all of this. If we're operating below our potential, no matter what our age, education, career, income level, or stage of life, it means that there's more of us to be realized. Awareness of unused potential is the first step toward anything positive, whether it's education, achievement, or personal growth in any form. In the dictionary potential is defined as: "existing in possibility; something that can develop or become actual." We need to think in terms of all the good things that actually are still out there "existing in possibility."

NO. 2 OF THE FABULOUS FOUR: IMAGINATION

Imagination is more important than knowledge, for knowledge is limited to all we now know and understand, while imagination embraces the entire world, and all there ever will be to know and understand.

—ALBERT EINSTEIN

THE ACTIVITY.   I handed out a sheet of paper with the word "imagination" and the Einstein quote at the top. These were the questions on the page, along with space for answers:

1. What is imagination?
2. What is the root word of imagination?
3. What well-known person do you most associate with imagination?
4. Who do you know personally who has a good imagination?
5. Why does Einstein say imagination is more important than knowledge?

Imagination is defined in the dictionary as "the act or power of forming a mental image of something." Some of the other definitions given are also enlightening: "creative ability," "resourcefulness," "ability to confront and deal with a problem," "the thinking or active mind." The root word is obviously "image." When we use our imaginations we're able to form images, or pictures, in our minds. And when we use them fully we can preview coming attractions in our lives. We can visualize, or "see" ourselves doing something we've never done before. The more frequently the images appear and the more vivid they are, the more likely we are to turn them into reality. *"We become what we think about."*

The name that came up the most often when students were asked to pick a well-known person associated with imagination was Walt Disney. Even though he died several years ago, his imagination continues to touch us in many ways. Some of the other names that came up often were Steven Spielberg, George Lucas, Bill Gates, Steve Jobs, and Robin Williams—two movie producers, two technology pioneers, and one comedian and actor. We tend to most associate famous people in entertainment and technology with imagination.

The more valuable discussion was about imaginative people we knew personally. We talked about all types of people—artists, novelists, musicians, architects, salespeople, teachers, pastors, business managers, entrepreneurs, athletes, coaches, homemakers, fashion designers, parents, decorators, columnists, and a host of others. During this discussion someone always came up with this observation: "We all have imaginations, and we can use them in anything we do." It's true that some people are more gifted than others in areas like art and music, but it doesn't mean that people without those particular talents aren't imaginative. Some people will say, as many of my students did, that they don't have much imagination, but that simply isn't true. It would be more accurate to say that they just don't *use* their imaginations as often as they could.

> *We are what we imagine ourselves to be.*
>
> —KURT VONNEGUT, JR.

Albert Einstein's name is practically synonymous with genius, and he's often referred to as the smartest person who ever lived. If he were alive today, he would strongly argue that point. He said imagination was not only more important than knowledge, but an important aspect of intellect. Discoveries, great and small, come from relaxing the mind, from play, from thinking about what's possible, from using the imagination. Every achievement in the history of the human race had the same starting place: the imagination.

> *Imagination will often carry us to worlds that never were, but without it we go nowhere.*
>
> —CARL SAGAN

An important aspect of imagination is what many psychologists call visualization—the ability to see ourselves doing something successfully before we actually try it. Athletes, inventors, builders, industrialists, leaders in business, and others have used this technique for many years. They have what is called a "vision," a clear picture in their minds about something important that they'll achieve in the future. The more clearly and more often they picture themselves doing it, the closer they move to fulfilling their dreams.

> *You must first clearly see a thing in your mind before you can do it.*
>
> —ALEX MORRISON

Two of the people who've done the most research in this area are Dr. Denis Waitley and Dr. Charles Garfield. Both have studied the relationship between use of the imagination and achievement. They've also written books and spoken frequently about the power of mental imagery. People who develop this skill not only envision themselves achieving, they habitually "rehearse" it in their minds. Garfield says people who learn to use their imaginations in this way have a "highly developed ability to imprint images of successful actions in the mind. They practice, mentally, specific skills and behaviors leading to those outcomes and achievements which they ultimately attain." Both he and Waitley say this skill has nothing to do with intelligence or special abilities. It's simply a matter of using something we've all been given—an imagination.

NO. 3 OF THE FABULOUS FOUR: OPPORTUNITY

> *Opportunity is all around us. If we seek it, we will find it.*
>
> —WYNN DAVIS

Opportunities multiply as they are seized.

—SUN TZU

THE ACTIVITY.   I handed out a sheet of paper with the word opportunity and these quotes at the top. On it, the students were asked to answer four questions:

1. What is opportunity?
2. Why do so many people never see the opportunities?
3. Why is the United States called "the land of opportunity"?
4. What are ten opportunities you see right now for your own life?

The definition of opportunity that we agreed upon was "the chance to do something." Merriam-Webster defines it this way: "a favorable juncture of circumstances; a good chance for advancement or progress." We discussed these two definitions at length, mainly because of the words "favorable" and "good" in them. There were always some students who said these dictionary definitions prove that circumstances have to be just right before an opportunity exists. Other students totally disagreed. They used the Wynn Davis quote above as their main arguing point: Opportunity is all around us, but we have to *look* for it.

They said this answered the second question about why people don't see the opportunities around them: they just don't look for them. They wait and hope for good things to happen in their lives instead of making them happen. It was always at this point that I put one of my favorite quotes on the board:

Success doesn't come to you, you go to it.

—MARVA COLLINS

Marva Collins is one of the greatest teachers of all time. She performed what many people in the media called "miracles" as an educator in Chicago. She made a positive and lasting impact on hundreds of kids from one of the roughest parts of town. One of the main things she did was to help those kids see the opportunities they'd never seen before. She convinced them if they'd change their outlook, get an education, and work hard, a whole new world would open up to them. That's exactly what happened. Many of those kids became doctors, lawyers, teachers, nurses, police officers, and business people. When interviewed as adults they all gave her credit for dramatically changing their lives. She helped them see opportunities that had always been there, but that they had never seen.

We do, indeed, live in "the land of opportunity." Why else would so many people in other parts of the world risk everything to come here? We have something that many other countries don't have: the opportunity to have a quality life. Unfortunately, many people born in this country never see it. It's harder to appreciate something if you've always had it. A former neighbor pointed this out to me several years ago. Gus moved into our neighborhood shortly after arriving from Indonesia. As I got to know him better, he talked often about how glad he was to be here and to know that his children had the same opportunity to succeed as everyone else did. He said, "People don't seem to understand how good they have it here. Every time I hear them complain about how bad things are, I just shake my head. Maybe you have to come from someplace else to truly see and appreciate the opportunities we have in this country."

How would you answer the fourth question? What are ten opportunities you see for *your* life right now? Most of my students fell into two groups in trying to answer this question. The first group had trouble coming up with ten. The other group had difficulty in limiting their list to ten. In other words, one group saw all kinds of opportunities; the other group needed some help. A comment made by one of my high-school kids during the discussion following this exercise will always stand out as the most insightful: "The truth is, we have hundreds of opportunities every day. We have opportunities to do just about anything. All we have to do is see them."

In 1988 a woman named Fran was in one of my evening classes at the university. Her list of the ten best opportunities she saw, which took her only a few minutes to write, is classic. With her permission, I shared it with all subsequent classes until my retirement from the classroom in 2001. It's also one of the few student assignments I saved in thirty-six years of teaching. Here are the ten opportunities, and the "bonus opportunity" that Fran saw:

1. The opportunity to learn as much as I need or want to
2. The opportunity to choose my own direction and achieve something in life
3. The opportunity to worship and honor God in countless ways
4. The opportunity to be a person of integrity and good character
5. The opportunity to choose, develop, and maintain a healthy attitude
6. The opportunity to care for others—family, friends, colleagues, strangers
7. The opportunity to make a contribution to a cause greater than myself
8. The opportunity to treasure my old friendships and to make new ones
9. The opportunity to enjoy and appreciate all that I have

10. The opportunity to grow and improve as a person every
     day of my life.

Bonus: The opportunity to see all my opportunities

NO. 4 OF THE FABULOUS FOUR: POSSIBILITIES

*If we did all the things we were capable of doing, we would
literally astound ourselves.*

—THOMAS EDISON

Our aspirations are our possibilities.

—ROBERT BROWNING

THE ACTIVITY.   I handed out a small slip of paper to each student in the class. It had nothing written on it. I told them that it
was a two-part activity. In part one they would write something on
one side of the paper after I asked them a preliminary question. It
was, "Would you agree that in the history of the human race there
have been thousands of great achievements?" They all agreed. I
then asked them to select any one of those thousands of great
achievements and write it down on the slip of paper. They had a
few questions of their own before they wrote. "Does it have to be
the greatest achievement?" was the first one. I said no, because we
would argue forever about which one was the greatest. My instructions were simply to select any one of them and write it down. I
assured them that they would not have to defend their choice.
Another question came up, one frequently asked at the high school
level: "Why are we doing this?" The answer was, "You'll see in a
minute. Trust me, this will be fun." And it was.

What I found interesting was that my high school students

wrote down essentially the same achievements that my adults at the university did. No matter what year this was done, the answers were almost identical. The achievement most frequently written on those slips of paper was, "Putting a man on the moon." Other frequent responses were: the automobile, the telephone (two that were very popular among teenagers), the light bulb, the airplane, television, DVDs, cell phones, music, art, the development of language, movies, the computer, the Internet, our highway system, books, the theater, the civil rights work of Martin Luther King, Jr., the charitable work of Mother Teresa, and advances in medicine. There were many others, but they were mentioned much less frequently.

This was always an enjoyable and uplifting experience because we were talking about human beings at their best—doing something for the good of mankind. There was always a buzz in the room when we shared our answers. Then came the inevitable question: "What's the second part?" I asked them to turn the slip of paper over so they could answer a different question on that side. I assured them that all the achievements they had written down were both great and life-changing. I asked them, "Did you know that each one of these achievements, no matter how different they are, had the same origins, the same starting place?" I got a few puzzled looks. I said, "I want to see if you can figure out what that starting place was. As a matter of fact, every achievement in the history of the human race, no matter how great or trivial, started there also. Please write down what you think it was."

Most of the students got it quickly. Others took more time, but they all got it. The two most common answers I received were, "They all started as an idea" and "They all started in someone's imagination." My response to their answers was, "Perfect!" I said, "Now I have one more question for you. Were the people who had these ideas thinking in terms of obstacles, limitations, and reasons why it couldn't be done, or were they thinking in terms of possibilities?" I didn't really need an answer. I pointed to the "Fabulous Four" signs surrounding the word THINKING. That's why they were there—to remind us that we have the POTENTIAL to do more with our lives, we've been given an IMAGINATION in which we can see the POSSIBILITIES, and we have OPPORTUNITY all around us.

Some of the world's greatest feats were accomplished by people not smart enough to know they were impossible.
                                        —DOUG LARSON

It takes someone with a vision of the possibilities to attain new levels of experience. Someone with the courage to live his dreams.
                                        —LES BROWN

Most people see what is, and never see what can be.
                                        —ALBERT EINSTEIN

Chapter Eight

RENEWAL

IT'S NEVER TOO LATE TO LEARN,
TO CHANGE, OR TO GROW.
MAKE ALL OF THEM
LIFELONG PURSUITS.

DEFINITIONS

*Renew: Restore to freshness, vigor; regenerate; to become new,
or as new.*

—MERRIAM-WEBSTER

*To develop skills, attitudes, habits of mind and the kinds of
knowledge and understanding that will be the instruments of
continuous change and growth.*

—JOHN W. GARDNER

RELATED WORDS/ VIRTUES	OPPOSITE WORDS/ FLAWS
Discover	Stagnate
Improve	Decay
Grow	Vegetate

8. Renewal

THE MEANING OF RENEWAL

*I think all human systems require continuous renewal. They
rigidify. They get stiff in the joints. They forget what they cared
about. The forces against it are nostalgia and the enormous
appeal of having things the way they have always been, appeals
to a supposedly happy past. But we've got to move on.*

—JOHN W. GARDNER

The quote above was written by one of my great personal heroes. John Gardner was at different times the architect of Medicare, Secretary of Health, Education, and Welfare, the founder of Common Cause, a prolific author and speaker, and an ethics professor in the Stanford Graduate School of Business until his death at eighty-nine in 2002. I had the privilege of hearing him speak at Stanford about a year before he died. He spoke that evening about *Self-Renewal,* a book he had written in 1963, which had been published in updated editions through 1995. Here was an eighty-eight-year-old man telling a large audience of people considerably younger than he was that renewal was central to a rewarding life.

At the beginning of his talk he read a passage from the fore-word of his book, something he had written almost forty years earlier. He said he was reading it because it was true long before he wrote it and that it will be true long after all of us are gone. He said we will be constantly "rediscovering the inescapable reality of change. Life and the world keep flowing and evolving." He said we all grasp that simple truth, but we're of two minds in deciding whether we like it or not. "There's something in us that fiercely resists change. And there's something else in us that welcomes it, finds it bracing, even seeks it out. It's the latter trait that keeps the species going." Then he closed the book, put it on a table, and said, "We have a choice: We can get hemmed in or liberated; we can suffer decay or celebrate renewal."

Stephen R. Covey, another of my heroes, has a different name for self-renewal in his groundbreaking book, *The 7 Habits of Highly Effective People.* His seventh habit is about renewal, and is called "Sharpen the Saw." He opens the chapter with a story about a man who had been trying to saw down a tree for more than five hours. An onlooker asks him why he doesn't take a break for a few minutes so he can sharpen his saw. The man replies: "I'm too busy sawing!" Whether we're busy or not, I think many of us too often forget the importance of taking a break to "sharpen the saw"—renew ourselves physically, mentally, socially, and spiritually. It does, in fact, make us much more "highly effective."

As I was laying out the title page for this chapter, I found several words that helped crystallize the meaning of renewal. But since I was only using three of them (discover, improve, grow), I had a number of excellent words left over. These words paint great pictures, and are so descriptive I didn't want to leave them out. Here are some wonderful "re" words that remind us what we do for ourselves when we decide to renew:

revive	restore	rejuvenate	refresh
reawaken	regenerate	revitalize	renovate
redevelop	recondition	reactivate	reinvent
re-create	redefine	reorganize	replenish
reinvigorate	recapture	recharge	rebirth
resurgence	revamp	rebuild	remodel
realign	refurbish	reconstruct	replace

GETTING OUT OF RUTS

Many people are in a rut, and a rut is nothing but a grave—
with both ends kicked out.

—VANCE HAVNER

Are you stuck in a rut and can't get out? Obviously, the only
way we can get out of a rut is by doing something different,
by changing.

—CHUCK GALLOZZI

In January 2003 I was in a Minneapolis TV studio for a brief interview about the publication of *Life's Greatest Lessons.* One of the anchors of the show, a warm and energetic woman named Sharon, had actually read the book beforehand and was genuinely enthused about it. She told me we'd only be on the air for about four minutes, and asked me to stay afterward for a little while because she wanted to ask me a few additional questions. While on the air, she focused her interview on chapter four of the book: "We live by choice, not by chance." She asked me what I thought were the most important choices we make. Limited by time constraints, I could only mention a few of those choices that were discussed in that first book. We choose our faith, we choose our character, we choose our attitudes, we choose our purpose, and we choose how much we'll learn.

After the interview and the program were over, Sharon and I resumed our talk about points in the book that had intrigued her. She said she noticed that I had mentioned the importance of learning in two key places. First, I listed it as one of the most important choices we make, then near the end of the book, in a chapter about the essentials of life, I mentioned it again. She read aloud the following passage from that chapter: "Have a passion to learn. The more you discover about life and the world, the more complete and fulfilled you'll become. Make it a lifelong process." She asked me, "Do you think you placed so much emphasis on learning because you're a teacher?" I answered, "No, I place so much emphasis on learning because I'm a learner. Learning not only keeps me out of ruts, it makes life more interesting, more enjoyable, and more rewarding."

For the next several minutes our conversation focused on ruts—getting in, staying in, getting out. Sharon had several questions about each. She figured that since I had written the book, I must be the expert with all the answers. But that was not the case. I simply told her that I equated ruts with the dull routines people get themselves into. They do the same mindless things over and over, and in the process, stifle themselves. I saw this in a lot of adults while growing up, and vowed that I would never let it happen to me. There was one basic reason—I didn't want to have a boring life.

When I was a junior in high school I read a short article in *Reader's Digest* that really got my attention. I can't remember the title of the article or the name of the author, but the content stuck. It was about ruts and boredom, and how to avoid them. It began with a story about a sign near the beginning of a long dirt highway in Alaska. It said, "Choose your rut carefully. You're going to be in it for a long time." Since that time I've seen many variations of this story. The location of the highway always changes, as does the amount of time you'll spend on it. But the point is always the same: once you get into a rut, you'll be there for a long time, and it's hard to get out. The author said there was a simple solution to the rut/boredom problem—learning. He said what we learn in school is only a warm-up, and that the most meaningful learning would come from reading, traveling, and meeting new people.

When I started college a few years later, that same point was strongly reinforced. During freshman orientation we heard a lot about the purpose of an education and about the purpose of life. Learning, whether in school or out of it, is our most important function. It starts shortly after birth and should continue until the end of life. Learning, or "the joy of discovery," as one of my professors called it, keeps us out of ruts, satisfies our natural curiosity, and adds meaning to our lives.

FOUR KINDS OF RENEWAL

Philosophers and sages throughout history have agreed that life has four important dimensions: physical, mental, social, and spiritual. In each category we need both nutrition and exercise, and in each category we need an occasional tune-up, or some degree of renewal. How much attention we pay to these four dimension of life, and how often we nurture them, varies greatly simply because we are so different in both our personalities and our experiences. As you look at the four categories, you might want to ask yourself the same two questions that I asked while outlining this chapter:

1. In which areas am I getting properly nourished?
2. In which areas do I need to devote more time and energy?

Because most of us don't do very well in maintaining a healthy balance in these four dimensions of life, we're reminded that we have work to do in one or more area. Here are our basic needs in each of the four:

1. Physical

BASIC NEEDS: Nutritional food, lots of water, proper rest, and regular exercise. Because this has been so well documented and publicized in recent years, I see no need to elaborate on it here. But I do want to make one important point regarding the human body. It isn't the most important part of us, but it's the vehicle that carries what *is* most important. If the vehicle breaks down, it usually has an adverse effect in one or more of the other three dimensions of life. The opposite is also true. When people upgrade their bodies through better care, they enhance the other dimensions of life. Have you ever known someone who stopped smoking, quit drinking, got off drugs, or lost a lot of weight? What do they most often say? "I feel like a new person, like I have a new lease on life!" They're happier, have more energy, and function better in all areas of life.

2. Mental

BASIC NEEDS.   The mind needs nutrition and exercise as much as the body does.

Nutrition. Just as we choose what goes into our bodies, we choose what goes into our minds. What's most helpful in keeping us out of those dreaded mental ruts is having completely new experiences on a regular basis. Travel satisfies this need in a variety of ways. For people unable to travel, there are other opportunities all around us. Taking a class in any subject of interest, learning a new skill, attending a lecture, or trying something we've never done before are a few examples of stimulating and feeding the mind.

Exercise. "Use it or lose it" is an expression with which we're all familiar. Nowhere is it more applicable than to the brain. Like a muscle in the body, it will atrophy if not exercised. In recent years doctors have published numerous articles in medical journals about the cost of mental laziness and the benefits of challenging ourselves. They report that board and card games that require memory work are enjoyable examples of this. They also mention doing puzzles that involve words or numbers as a way of exercising the mind. The opportunities to learn something new and stimulate the brain daily are limitless. Each time we do, we renew ourselves and add meaning to our lives.

3. Social

BASIC NEEDS: People—family, friends, colleagues, community. What is the harshest of all punishments administered to the worst of the worst in our prisons? It isn't the death penalty, it isn't the denial of privileges, it isn't a beating, it isn't hard labor. It's solitary confinement—the total separation from other people. It denies a person one of his or her most basic needs: human contact. Virtually everyone understands this. But how do we renew ourselves socially? By making new friends. I'm not suggesting that we dump old friends and/or family members, but I *am* suggesting that we get into social ruts when we never make any changes in this part of our lives.

There's an old expression that claims: "There's no such thing as a stranger. There are only friends we haven't met." Like most old expressions, it's true. Old friends are one of the great comforts of life—treasure them. But a new friend is one of the great joys of life. Because I travel extensively to speak, I'm frequently asked the same question: "What do you like most about your traveling and speaking?" Some people even venture a guess as to what it is: meals in great restaurants (along with many meals in not-so-great restaurants), staying in fancy hotels (along with staying in many not-so-fancy hotels), new and exciting places (along with some old and not-so-exciting places), seeing famous landmarks (along with seeing highways, factories, and farms), making money (along with making no money). Fortunately, I've been blessed withall of these experiences, but my answer would be, "None of the above." The greatest reward of what I do has been making new friends. I don't mean just for the duration of my visit, but for life. I keep regular contact with many of them, and make a point to see them as often as I can. Why? Because they've enriched my life, and they continue to do so. You don't have to travel anywhere to make new friends. There are wonderful people in our communities, at work, and in our places of worship who are potential new friends. They can help renew us by adding both joy and meaning to our lives.

4, Spiritual

BASIC NEEDS. The holy scriptures of all faiths, instruction, books, and prayer. This is a dimension of life that's most often ignored. A former great Secretary-General of the United Nations and recipient of the Nobel Peace Prize wrote:

> On the bookshelf of life, God is a useful work of reference, always at hand but seldom consulted.
>
> —DAG HAMMARSKJÖLD

This spiritual aspect of life is too important to be ignored, whether or not we belong to a particular faith. Most people acknowledge that there's a power much greater than us. While this higher power has been ascribed several different names, I honor it as God. Because people have different belief systems, we honor and worship God in different ways. But it's God who ties us all together as humans, gives us a free will, and asks us to respect and love one another.

We can learn and renew ourselves spiritually by being open to what all the great religious leaders and philosophers have taught us about being human. No one faith has a monopoly on the world's wisdom. I'm not a Buddhist, a Confucian, or a Taoist, but I benefit greatly from the teachings of Buddha, Confucius, and Lao-tzu. I'm neither a Mormon nor a Jew, but I've been deeply enriched by the insight and understanding of Stephen Covey and Rabbi Harold Kushner, two of my favorite authors. Most of the key principles of these and other spiritual writers are consistent with, and reinforce, the teachings of my Christian faith.

The way we meet our most basic spiritual needs is the same way we renew ourselves spiritually—by turning to the scriptures, receiving instruction, reading books that illuminate the scriptures, and praying. Because I feel so strongly that praying and reading the holy books are two of the most important and wisest choices we can make, I've devoted a chapter to each near the end of this book.

THE JOYS OF LIFELONG LEARNING

The process of keeping the mind alive and growing is as perpetual and continual a process as that of keeping the human body alive. But whereas there are limits to the body's growth, the mind, unlike the body, can grow every year of our lives. The only condition of its growth is that it be fed and exercised.

—MORTIMER ADLER

Mortimer Adler is yet another of my heroes, for a number of reasons. He was a great scholar, philosopher, educational theorist, and prolific author. One of his passions was studying the lives and teachings of the great philosophers, and then writing about them in such a way that everyone could understand. He's often been called "The People's Philosopher." His other great contribution was in the field of lifelong learning. He researched, wrote, and spoke about it more than anyone in history. It was his belief that school, no matter how far we go in it, is only the beginning, and that what we learn there barely scratches the surface. Real learning occurs only in our adult years after we've completed our formal schooling.

The main point that Adler makes about lifelong learning is that it is an absolute essential for leading a full life. He stressed that education was a lifelong process because learning never reaches a terminal point. He said we die inside, even though our bodies are still alive, when we stop learning. We also become bored and boring. The solution is constant renewal, or learning. Adler had strong convictions that continual learning resulted in personal growth in all dimensions of life: spiritual, moral, and emotional, as well as mental. "As long as one remains alive and healthy, learning can go on—and should," he said. If we feed and exercise the mind properly, we increase our energy and enthusiasm for life, find more meaning and joy, make ourselves more interesting, and grow in wisdom.

[We] should be able to look forward not only to growing up, but also to continued growth in all human dimensions throughout life. All should aspire to make as much of their powers as they can.

—MORTIMER ADLER

Early in my teaching career I was having a lunchtime discussion with one of my colleagues, an outstanding high school English teacher. We were sharing our feelings about how much we loved our jobs. She said, "One of the greatest things about it is that I learn so much every day. Whether I'm preparing lesson plans or teaching, I'm always learning something new. Just think about how many years we have ahead of us in which we'll get paid for continuing to learn." Because both of us were committed to learning as a lifelong process, we agreed that it was one of the great fringe benefits of our profession. We both tried to convince our students that learning in school was only the beginning, but at their age, the concept of lifelong learning was difficult to grasp or appreciate.

That was not the case for my adult students at the University of San Francisco. They proved over and over that Adler's point about adults being better learners was true. Most of my students were in their thirties, forties, and fifties. All of them had gone to high school, then took a year or two of community college, and then went to work. Many of them had been out of school for several years. Because many were in management positions, their employers wanted them to have four-year degrees and offered to pay the tuition. They returned to school with a certain amount of fear. But once they realized that all their classmates had the same concerns, they relaxed and became what I called "hungry learners." Many surprised themselves by being much better students than they had been in previous years.

Because they were adults who were genuinely excited about learning, the idea of lifelong learning was an easier sell than it was at the high school. I had the same students throughout a series of courses, so we spent several consecutive months together. I started the curriculum by introducing Mortimer Adler and his theories on adult learning, and handed out some brief essays he had written on the topic. Because Adler had written so passionately and eloquently about a lifelong education, and because my students were discovering the joy of learning for the first time, it was an easy sell.

One of the many rewards of teaching is keeping contact with former students, many of whom become dear friends. Because I emphasized it so much, they always let me know they're "still learning" and "still renewing" themselves. That's music to a teacher's ears. The best part, though, is hearing the genuine excitement in their voices and their usage of the term "joy of learning." One of my former adult students seemed to capture the feelings of many when she sent me the following e-mail a few years ago:

> Hello Life-Long Learning Guy,
>
> Although I greatly appreciated how much I learned while in your classes, I didn't really believe you when you said we'd learn even more and find it even more enjoyable *after* we got our degrees. I thought I needed to give my brain a rest after finishing the program, so I kind of "vegged" for a while. But that only lasted a few weeks. Then I began to understand why you shared with us what John Gardner and Mortimer Adler had to say about renewal and life-long learning. LEARNING IS AWESOME! AND IT IS A JOY! You'd be so proud of me if you could see the many ways in which I'm continuing my education. Learning and renewal really do add more meaning and joy! Your life-long student,
>
> Barbara

THE MAGIC OF BOOKS

*All that mankind has done, thought, gained, or been, it is lying
as in magic preservation in the pages of books. They are the
chosen possession of men.*

—THOMAS CARLYLE

There are many ways in which we can learn without
reading, but books still provide us with one of the
least expensive and most mobile forms of education
we'll ever have. Since you're reading this one, I'll assume that you
also treasure books. There's no need to convince you, only remind
you, that books are among our greatest possessions. The quote
above is near the top of my all-time favorites. It used to be carved
in large letters into the stone wall outside the old library in my
hometown of Redwood City, California. I loved driving by it and
reading it often. It was like seeing an old friend. I want to end this
chapter by sharing a few more quotes that all book lovers will
appreciate:

*It is chiefly through books that we enjoy intercourse with
superior minds, and these invaluable means of communication
are in the reach of all. In the best books, great men talk to us,
give us their most precious thoughts, and pour their souls
into ours.*

—WILLIAM ELLERY CHANNING

*Books are the food of youth, the delight of old age; the ornament
of prosperity, the refuge and comfort of adversity; a delight at
home, and no hindrance abroad; companions by night, in
traveling, in the country.*

—CICERO

Books are the quietest and most constant of friends: they are the most accessible and wisest of counselors, and the most patient of teachers.

—CHARLES W. ELIOT

There is more treasure in books than in all the pirates' loot on Treasure Island.

—WALT DISNEY

A good book is the best of friends, the same today and forever.

—MARTIN TUPPER

A home without books is a body without a soul.

—CICERO

A wonderful thing about a book, in contrast to a computer screen, is that you can take it to bed with you.

—DANIEL J. BOORSTEIN

When I have a little money, I buy books; and if any is left, I buy food and clothes.

—ERASMUS

At the university I taught a series of six courses in organizational behavior to the same group of students. Throughout the curriculum, I recommended a wide variety of books on philosophy, leadership, biography, business management, psychology, educational theory, faith, and personal growth. The program they were in required extensive reading and writing, so I knew they wouldn't be able to read the books I recommended until afterward when their "real education" would begin. Since these book suggestions were not part of the assigned curriculum, I really didn't have any idea how many I'd made. I found out at the end of the program. One woman in the class had written down every book I'd suggested, typed up her list, and gave a copy to everyone at our last meeting. It had more than a hundred books on it. One of the things I'd had my students do earlier in the program was write both professional and personal goals. She said one of her goals was to read every one of those books. Several of the other students also expressed appreciation for the reading suggestions, and many vowed to read most of them so their education would continue.

> *The more that you read, the more things you will know.*
> *The more that you learn, the more places you'll go.*
>
> —DR. SEUSS

> *I cannot live without books.*
>
> —THOMAS JEFFERSON

Chapter Nine

COURAGE

IT TAKES COURAGE TO SAY "YES"
TO LIFE. MAKE IT A DAILY
COMMITMENT.

DEFINITIONS

Courage: Mental or moral strength to venture, persevere, and withstand danger, fear, or difficulty.

—MERRIAM-WEBSTER

Courage is resistance to fear, mastery of fear—not absence of fear.

—MARK TWAIN

RELATED WORDS/ VIRTUES	OPPOSITE WORDS/ FLAWS
Honor	Wimpishness
Strength	Fear
Fortitude	Cowardice

9. Courage

EVERY DAY IS A TEST OF COURAGE

Courage is not limited to the battlefield or the Indianapolis 500 or bravely catching a thief in your house. The real tests of courage are much quieter. They are inner tests, like remaining faithful when no one's looking, like enduring pain when the room is empty, like standing alone when you're misunderstood.

—CHARLES SWINDOLL

We often equate courage with valor, bravery, gallantry, and heroism. It conjures up images of great martyrs like Joan of Arc, patriots like the people who declared our independence and fought in the American Revolution, reformers like Mahatma Gandhi, civil rights leaders like Nelson Mandela and Martin Luther King, Jr., and other well-known heroes throughout history. The courage of these people has always been honored and celebrated. It's the best known and most admired of many types of courage. But we need to be reminded that there are other types of courage that are equally important. One of them is "everyday courage."

Everyday courage has few witnesses. But yours is no less noble because no drum beats for you and no crowds shout your name.

—ROBERT LOUIS STEVENSON

Life is hard, and not always fair. Whether we like it or not, that's the way things are. This sometimes harsh reality leaves us with a choice: we can snivel and whine about it and act like wimps when life deals out some hard blows, or we can accept it as a challenge and show the courage to make the most of it. More than a hundred years ago a famous playwright wrote *Man and Superman*. In it, he gives us some great advice for dealing with the hardships of life. He says we should be . . .

> . . . *a force of nature instead of a feverish selfish little clod of ailments and grievances complaining that the world will not devote itself to making you happy.*
>
> —GEORGE BERNARD SHAW

In more modern times, a well known advice-giver said something similar:

> *If I were asked to give what I consider the single most useful bit of advice for all humanity it would be this: Expect trouble as an inevitable part of life and when it comes, hold your head high, look it squarely in the eye, and say, "I will be bigger than you. You cannot defeat me."*
>
> —ANN LANDERS

Life *is* hard and life *is* often unfair and we *can* expect trouble. But that doesn't mean we have to let it defeat us. Digging down, finding strength, and standing up to hardship can be one of the great rewards and joys of life. It takes courage—the everyday kind.

THE HIGHEST FORM OF COURAGE IS SAYING "YES" TO LIFE

> *I understand the Courage to Be as the courage to say "yes" to life in spite of all the negative elements in human existence—in spite of man's finitude, which means his coming from nothing*

and going to nothing, to die. . . . It takes courage to see in the
reality around us and in us something ultimately positive and
meaningful and live with it, even love it. Loving life is perhaps
the highest form of the courage to be.

—PAUL TILLICH

I discovered the above quote more than thirty years ago, and it remains one of my favorites. Why? Because it addresses one of the central issues of life. It reminds us that it takes courage daily to find real meaning and purpose in our lives—and this leads to joy. Paul Tillich was a highly revered German philosopher and theologian who spent the last ten years of his life (1956–65) as a professor at Harvard and the University of Chicago. Among his many books was *The Courage to Be,* published in 1952. It's one of those books a reader never forgets. No author has ever said so much in four words: **SAY YES TO LIFE.** That simple phrase seems to crystallize what ancient philosophers and sages of all faiths and cultures have been telling us for thousands of years—our life on earth has meaning and an ultimate purpose. When we come to understand that life is a balancing act between good and evil, and we work our way through the hardship and suffering that come with it, we eventually discover and appreciate the joy that surrounds us. The most basic requirement is courage.

Tillich reminds us that while neither birth nor death are choices, everything in between is. And in spite of life's many "negative elements," we're challenged to make the most of it under all circumstances. If we don't have the courage to do this, we'll never find the real meaning of our lives. And we'll never become the fully alive people we're capable of being. He says courage is the "vital strength" we need to rise above the hardships and sufferings of life and find "something ultimately positive and meaningful."

MORAL COURAGE

It is curious—curious that physical courage should be so common in the world, and moral courage so rare.

—MARK TWAIN

Mark Twain made the above remark more than 150 years ago. He and others of his time expressed concern about the decline in morality they were witnessing as our country was growing stronger. As opportunities to attain wealth and other symbols of outward success increased, virtues like honesty and integrity declined. I wonder what Twain and his contemporaries would think if they were with us today. There seems to have been somewhat of a moral meltdown in recent years. It was rampant in the eighties, when the ethos of many was "greed is good." But it was even more prevalent in the late nineties and early 2000s when we learned almost daily about a new corporate scandal. Many of the people who were involved said later that they "just got caught up" in what was going on around them. One of the young men who pleaded guilty in the Enron scandal lamented in court, "I let myself get sucked into this. I didn't have the courage to stand up for what's right."

Standing up for what's right is a good definition of moral courage. It could range from an elementary school child who stands up to and reports a bully, to a teenager who refuses to cave in under pressure from peers to do something wrong, to an adult at work who stands up to a supervisor who's asking him or her to do something unethical. In all such cases, there's a risk of suffering a loss as a result of doing the right thing. Dr. Judith V. Jordan, a professor at Harvard Medical School, speaking at the Stone Center at Wellesley College, said this type of courage "is the capacity to act meaningfully and with integrity in the face of acknowledged vulnerability." Dr. Rushworth M. Kidder, the head of the Institute for Global Ethics, and the author of a book entitled *Moral Courage,* writes in his "President's Letter" that "it's about facing mental challenges that could harm one's reputation, emotional well-being, self-esteem, or other characteristics. These challenges, as the term implies, are deeply connected with our moral sense—our core moral values."

A more specific definition of moral courage can be found in the book *The Mystery of Courage,* written by a University of Michigan professor of law:

> *For us, moral courage has come to mean the capacity to*
> *overcome the fear of shame and humiliation in order to admit*
> *one's mistakes, to confess a wrong, to reject evil conformity, to*
> *denounce injustice, and also to defy immoral or imprudent orders.*
>   —WILLIAM IAN MILLER

Located in the Baltimore suburb of Brooklandville, Maryland, is St. Paul's School for Boys. In addition to having a mission statement and clearly stated policies, the Lower School has a prayer. Students ask for divine help in some areas in which they're daily challenged: clean words, clean thoughts, hard work, fair play, being kind, forgiving others, helping others, and doing good every day. It's a prayer that adults need just as much as young school children do. It has a single line in it that reminds us of a challenge that we face almost daily:

HELP ME TO STAND FOR THE HARD RIGHT AGAINST THE EASY WRONG.

I came across the prayer while reading an article about moral courage, and this one line seemed to jump off the page. I couldn't help thinking about how many times throughout the various stages of life we find ourselves in situations often referred to as moral dilemmas. I also couldn't help thinking about how often we take the easy way out. It's simply easier to walk away and "not get involved" than it is to stand up for a moral or ethical principle. It takes courage to do the right thing when there's a chance that we'll suffer unfairly because of it. We need to remind ourselves often of one of the greatest lessons of history: Good triumphs, in things both big and small, only when people show the courage to stand up for it.

It often helps us to better understand and more diligently practice a virtue when we clearly see the weakness or flaw that is the opposite of it. On the title page of this chapter one of the words listed as the opposite of courage is cowardice. It's one of the ugliest words in our language. Merriam-Webster describes a *coward* as "one who shows disgraceful fear or timidity." It isn't having fear that's bad. We all have it from time to time. But having "disgraceful fear" is another thing altogether. We disgrace ourselves when we become morally lazy or morally timid, or both. We take the easy way out when we're called to take a stand for what's good and right.

THE MOTHER OF ALL VIRTUES

Courage is the first of human qualities because it makes all the others possible.

—ARISTOTLE

Courage is not just one of the virtues, but the form of every virtue at the testing point.

—C. S. LEWIS

A number of philosophers and influential writers throughout history have claimed that courage is the mother of all virtues, that we can't practice the others without having it first. There's substantial evidence to support their claim. Much of it is provided by Rushworth Kidder, who has conducted research on universal values and virtues for many years. In the "President's Letter" cited above, he writes, "Moral courage plays itself out daily, hourly. . . . Without it, our brightest virtues rust from lack of use. With it, we build piece by piece a more ethical world."

What are the "brightest virtues"? Kidder spoke at length about them in a keynote address at a recent Character Education Partnership conference. He and his associates have asked this questionhundreds of thousands of people all over the globe. They represent a great variety of cultures, age groups, races, religions, and lifestyles. The five traits they most consistently select as the "core moral values" are: respect, responsibility, honesty, compassion, and fairness. At the root of each of them is courage. As Aristotle said, courage makes our other good qualities possible.

Every society throughout history has shown a concern for right and wrong, good and evil. And every person throughout history has been faced with difficult choices—moral and ethical dilemmas. It's not easy to be consistently respectful, responsible, honest, compassionate, and fair. Moral courage is what enables us to face up to these daily challenges. The more often we choose it, the more often we draw from it, the more we strengthen it and our other virtues.

COMFORT ZONES AND THE COURAGE TO CHANGE

Move out of your comfort zone. You can only grow if you are willing to feel awkward and uncomfortable when you try something new.

—BRIAN TRACY

I had some favorite sayings during my many years in the classroom. And because repetition is the mother of learning, I deliberately said them often. There were always a few students who thought my memory was starting to go, and they reminded me that I had "said that before." My response was, "In teaching, we call that reinforcement. The more I say it, the more likely you are to remember it." Since I regarded personal growth as an integral part of each course I taught, this is one of the sayings my students heard most frequently:

"YOU'LL NEVER GROW UNTIL YOU TAKE SOME STEPS OUTSIDE YOUR COMFORT ZONE."

Because I've always been a firm believer in visible reminders, I had several large signs in the room which further reinforced my major points. One of them looked like this:

COMFORT ZONE NO PARKING

The first time my students heard the phrase and saw me point at the sign, they weren't sure of its meaning. They asked for both a definition of "comfort zone" and some examples of taking steps outside of it. My definition of comfort zone is this: a personal space, or way of doing things, in which we get comfortable, whether it's good or bad for us. Comfort zones are often related to habits, and sometimes to ruts. There's no anxiety or fear or risk in our comfort zones, so it's easy to stay in them. There are examples all around us. Here are a few on the negative side: smoking, laziness, staying in bad relationships, overeating, complaining, being timid, excessive TV viewing, overspending, and being close-minded. Why do people continue to do these things even when they know they're harmful? The answer is simple: It's more comfortable to repeat a negative action than it is to give it up. Changing requires courage, risk, discomfort, and hard work.

One of the comfort zones we get into has to do with speech patterns. We often develop verbal habits without even knowing it, and then they become part of our everyday routine. Early in my teaching career I noticed that one verbal rut young people get into is constantly putting each other down. Unfortunately, it's a big part of our youth culture. It was always disturbing to me, whether the kids were "just kidding" or being serious. In the early 1970s I had a long discussion about this with a wonderful group of high school seniors in my psychology class. I always devoted a lot of time and energy at the beginning of the school year to creating a good classroom environment. My point with the kids was this: "Putdowns poison the atmosphere."

When I asked them if they affirmed and built people up as much as they put them down, I got a two-word answer: "No way." My obvious question had only one word: "Why?" They agreed with me that putting people down was part of the culture, that it was a pattern easy to slip into, and that it wasn't conducive to a healthy environment. I asked them if they were willing to try to reverse it, and to spend some time at the beginning of each class affirming one another. The first student who responded captured the feelings of everyone in the class. He said, "Oh, that would be awkward and embarrassing." In other words, building someone up would be much harder to do than putting someone down. Clearly, it was a comfort zone issue.

I asked them if they were willing to work their way out of their negative comfort zones in the hope of moving into a new and more positive comfort zone. They said they were, so we took a few minutes each day to issue some sincere compliments and expressions of appreciation. It was, indeed, "awkward and embarrassing" at first, but they stuck with it, and gradually became comfortable using more affirming language. I'll never forget the kids in that class. They were trailblazers. They had the courage to come out of their comfort zones, they took the risk of feeling awkward and embarrassed by trying something new, and they proved that even teenagers could develop positive speech patterns. They also helped me start a valuable tradition that was part of every class I taught until my retirement in 2001.

At the suggestion of the students, we put up another sign:

> ## NO PUTDOWNS
> ---
> ## COMPLIMENTS SPOKEN HERE

RISK AND FAILURE ARE ASPECTS OF COURAGE

What would we be if we had no courage to attempt anything?
—Vincent van Gogh

The greatest risk is the risk of riskless living.
—Stephen R. Covey

I'm not going to suggest here that we should take wild and reckless risks with either our lives or our life savings, and I'm not going to suggest that failure isn't painful. But I *am* suggesting that risk and failure are essential aspects of life and growth, and necessary steps for any type of success. No one has ever been successful in everything he or she tried, and no one has escaped the sting of failure. The people who understand this take sensible risks and are not afraid to fail, accepting it as part of the process. They're also the people who find the most meaning and joy in their lives.

If you look up *risk* in the dictionary, you're likely to find words like these to define it: *danger, hazard, peril,* and *loss.* My Merriam-Webster defines risk this way: "possibility of loss or hazard; peril." While the likelihood of loss is always present when we take a risk, there's also a positive aspect to it. If you look up *risk* in a thesaurus, you'll find additional words like these: *chance, probability, possibility,* and *venture.* Yes, there's a chance you'll suffer a loss, but there's also a chance that you'll make progress toward an important goal. Yes, risk involves the possibility or probability of loss, but it also involves the possibility or probability of success. You can't have one without the other. The word that best describes both sides of taking a risk is *venture.* It can probably best be summed up in the time-honored maxim: "Nothing ventured, nothing gained."

We fail far more often by timidity than by over-daring.
—DAVID GRAYSON

In *Life's Greatest Lessons* I wrote that it's OK to fail—everyone else has. The bottom line is that everyone experiences failure, and some people fail many times until they finally "get it." I can't even count how many times I've failed at various things. But it's perfectly OK because failure is a fact of life, part of the process, and no one escapes it. It isn't *whether* we fail that matters; it's *how* we fail. The difference between the people who succeed in life and the ones who have difficulty creating success isn't found in the number of times they fail. It's found in the courage they have to take a risk, and it's found in what they do *after* they fail.

Failure is one of life's greatest teachers. That is, if we choose to learn from it rather than be crushed by it. If we have the courage to venture out of our comfort zones, to risk a loss, and to confront failure, we just may end up being better and stronger. If we do fail we're left with an important choice: give up and quit or learn from our mistakes and move on. Our failures in life, as painful as they are, can be our most valuable learning experiences and our greatest source of renewed strength.

COURAGE IS ITS OWN REWARD

There are a number of good things that happen to us when we tap into our resources and act on our courage, especially our moral courage. Here are a few:

1. *We become mentally stronger.* Every courageous act, even a small one, increases our confidence to stand up for what is right.
2. *We increase our self-esteem.* Any act of courage has an exhilarating effect. Standing up for what's right enhances us at the very core of our existence. It increases our feelings of self-worth.
3. *We help and inspire others.* Acts of courage often arouse other people. When they see someone around them act courageously, they're more likely to do the same.

4. *We create better communities.* No matter where we are—home, work, school, or other places—an act of courage enhances the moral climate. It helps increase awareness in others and stirs them to action.

5. *We become persons of integrity.* This is the best reward of all, because courage helps us become complete. Although integrity is closely related to honesty, it's really a much broader term. It comes from the word *integral,* which means "essential to completeness." Honesty and courage are essential to developing integrity.

Whether you be a man or a woman you will never do anything in this world without courage. It is the greatest quality of the mind next to honor.

—JAMES ALLEN

Chapter Ten

EXCELLENCE

REAL SUCCESS COMES FROM HAVING
HIGH STANDARDS.
ALWAYS GIVE YOUR BEST.

DEFINITIONS

Excellent: very good of its kind; eminently good; first-class.

—MERRIAM-WEBSTER

Excellence is doing ordinary things extraordinarily well.

—JOHN W. GARDNER

RELATED WORDS/ VIRTUES	OPPOSITE WORDS/ FLAWS
Exceptional	Apathetic
Admirable	Mediocre
First-rate	Lazy

10. Excellence

No one measures up to the present opportunity until he has put his BEST into each operation every day. It may not be easy to do but it is well worth the price.

—J. C. Penney

How would you answer the above question? I asked it at the beginning of each school year after pointing to yet another sign in my classroom. It said:

ALWAYS GIVE YOUR BEST

I asked both my teenage and adult students this question. The responses from both groups were remarkably similar over a period of more than thirty years. The first one was always another question like, "What do you mean?" So, I tried to make the question a little more specific: "What percentage of the time while you're awake do you give the best you have?" Then came another question: "At what?" "At everything," I answered. This was followed by a few moments of silence, which was a good sign. I would say, "Good, I can hear you thinking."

This question *does* make people think. It always prompted a long and valuable discussion about what it means to "give your best" before anyone would venture a specific answer. Some legitimate questions came up during these discussions. They could be summed up this way: How do you give your best when you're watching TV or a movie, resting, talking on the phone, reading a newspaper or magazine, partying, going out to dinner, walking the dog, attending a concert or athletic event, and so on? Someone invariably made the comment that if we always "gave our best" during these kinds of activities we'd be too intense and stressed out and would drive everyone around us nuts—including the dog.

Obviously, we needed to reach an agreement on what it means to "always give your best." But first, we had to establish what it *doesn't* mean. It was important to point out that it has nothing to do with being too intense or stressed out. In fact, those are times when we *can't* be at our best. Giving our best doesn't mean working eighteen hours a day, giving up rest, eating poorly while on the run, being preoccupied, and shutting out family and friends. That's virtually the opposite—it's when we're at our worst. Giving our best means two things:

1. Setting high personal standards
2. Living up to those standards regardless of circumstances

You can be giving your best while relaxing or socializing—which are absolutely essential activities—as long as you're being consistent with the standards you've set. This is what it really means to always give your best:

> **WHEREVER YOU ARE,**
> **WHATEVER YOU'RE DOING,**
> **WHOEVER YOU'RE WITH,**
> **GIVE THE BEST YOU HAVE.**

Once this was established, we got back to answering the original question: How often do you give your best? The answers ranged from 25 to 95 percent, with the adults giving significantly higher numbers. Keep in mind that my adult students were pro-

fessional people, well established in their careers, and highly moti-
vated. After everyone shared their numbers and briefly explained
how they were calculated, I asked another question: "Why would
you ever want to give less than the best you have?" This was always
followed by another long period of silence. Again, it was the sound
of thinking, and I loved it.

The most common answers I received were: not feeling well,
tired, in a bad mood, and lazy. My response to the first two was
that if you're tired or not feeling well you can still give your best
under those particular circumstances. My response to the other two
was that they were lame excuses. Keep in mind that I did this in
good humor and with a smile, but still meant what I said. Bad
moods and laziness are choices. We can talk ourselves out of bad
moods and we can choose to not be lazy. In truth, there *is* no good
answer to this question. There never was and never will be a good
reason for not giving the best that's within us.

Life will always be less than it can be when we don't give our best.
And life will always be more fulfilling when we give the best we have.

To make a point, these are some of the questions I posed to
my students:

- When in an airplane, do you want the pilot to do the best he can?
- When taking a class, do you want the teacher to do the best she can?
- When playing sports, do you want your teammates to do the best they can?
- When attending a concert, do you want the singer to do the best he can?
- When at work, do you want your boss to do the best she can?
- When driving a car, do you want the other drivers to do the best they can?
- When in your place of worship, do you want the leader to do the best he can?

- When eating in a restaurant, do you want the chef to do the best she can?
- When running a business, do you want your employees to do the best they can?
- When someone's working on your home, do you want him to do the best he can?
- When someone's managing your finances, do you want her to the best she can?

I asked my students what the above questions had in common. It didn't take long before it dawned on most of them that when other people are doing something for us, we want them to give their best. Why? Because it's in *our* best interest. It's also in our best interest to give the best we can under all circumstances. Why? Because there's a basic and simple law of life that tells us:

**OUR REWARDS IN LIFE WILL ALWAYS BE IN
DIRECT PROPORTION
TO WHAT WE GIVE TO LIFE.**

Several years ago I had a senior high school student named Brian. He stayed after class one day to talk to me. He asked, "Do you remember that day about a month ago when you asked us why we would ever want to give less than the best we have?" I told him that I remembered it well because I asked it every year of all of my students. He said, "Well, it's been over a month now, and I can't get it out of my head. You know what, there really *isn't* any reason not to give your best." He said he didn't believe me when I said there was no good answer to that question, but after thinking about it for more than a month, and trying to come up with one, he had arrived at the same conclusion. How I wished all of my students would do such heavy thinking! Then he said, "You know, if you have something to do, you might as well give it your best shot." I couldn't have said it better myself.

About twelve years later I heard from Brian again. He sent an e-mail to tell me about his new career and his upcoming marriage. He said they were two of the most important goals he had written while in my class, and he wanted to share with me that he could now check them off. Nothing pleases a teacher more than hearing things like these from former students. Then he asked me if I remembered that day when we had talked about reasons for not giving our best. I told him that I'd never forget it. It was one of those signature moments in a long teaching career that overflowed with blessings. He said, "That question changed my life. I'm where I am today because I *always* give my best. Life is so much better because of it. I hope you're still asking that question." I was.

Although I'm no longer in the classroom, I continue to ask this question hundreds of times each year—in schools of kids, teachers, and parents, at conferences, in churches, in businesses, and in service organizations. And, yes, I ask it of myself regularly. How often do *you* give your best?

SETTING HIGH STANDARDS IN FOUR IMPORTANT AREAS

Setting high standards makes every day and every decade worth looking forward to.

—STEVE BRUNKHORST

A number of years ago I was giving a talk to a large group of college students about the real meaning of success and about the most important choices we make in life. As I always do, I urged them to look for the good, especially within themselves, to make good choices, to set high standards, and to always give their best. During the question-and-answer period that followed, one of the students prefaced her question by pointing out that life has many aspects. Then she asked, "Could you be a little more specific about setting high standards? In which areas of life are they most important?" The question threw me off a little at first simply because it had never been asked before. It made me realize that my presentation would have been more effective with some concrete examples of setting high standards.

I thought for a moment, and then answered, "There are four which come immediately to mind: first, character, particularly honesty; second, how we treat other people; third, work ethic; and fourth, personal growth and development." I explained that when I was their age I had high standards in only one of these areas: work ethic. I had always been a hard worker, but learned that hard work alone doesn't make us successful. The quality of my life improved immeasurably after I learned the importance of setting a higher standard in the other three areas as well. I urged the students to do the same. I remember thinking at the time that I had probably left out some important categories, but those were the best I could come up with under the circumstances. I mulled over my answer for the next several days, wondering what else should have been included. Happily, I came to the conclusion that it was a pretty decent answer. I couldn't come up with any other areas of life that were more important.

Let's examine each of these four categories in which having high standards leads to increased fulfillment and joy.

1. Character and Honesty

Character is the sum of those qualities which make a man a good man and a woman a good woman.

—THEODORE ROOSEVELT

Honesty is the first chapter in the book of wisdom.
                                    —Thomas Jefferson

In the character education movement we promote a wide variety of core virtues such as respect, responsibility, attitude, self-discipline, caring, kindness, hard work, and honesty. All of these are admirable traits. But if the last one—honesty—isn't in place, the others don't mean a thing. I want to repeat something here that I wrote several years ago in the chapter about honesty in *Life's Greatest Lessons.* "You'll never be truly successful unless everything you do is undergirded with honesty and integrity. You'll never know peace of mind and you'll never enjoy feelings of self-worth unless truthfulness is deeply embedded in your character." In other words, there's no such thing as good character without honesty.

As important as honesty is, it's one of the most difficult subjects to write about, teach about, or even talk about. One of the reasons is that most people are uncomfortable with the subject. We've all done dishonest things, some of them at great cost, and we've all been burned by the dishonesty of other people. It's an almost daily challenge to be honest in all things, so people often take moral shortcuts. What makes the challenge even greater is a prevailing belief that "everyone's doing it." This is especially true when it comes to expense accounts, insurance claims, and income taxes.

There's also a mistaken, but common, belief that no one is honest all the time. I say it's a mistaken belief because there are countless people who lead lives of impeccable integrity. Unfortunately, we don't hear about them very much because everyday honesty and integrity aren't celebrated in the media. These people go quietly about their lives, conduct themselves with honor, and earn the respect of everyone. They're living proof that we *can* be honest in all things.

These are people of character, which Merriam-Webster defines as "moral excellence and firmness." They lead more satisfying lives because they continually reap the rewards of honesty and integrity: a solid reputation, the respect and admiration of others, peace of mind, strong relationships based on trust, feelings of self-respect and authenticity.

2. How We Treat Other People

Treat other people exactly as you'd like to be treated by them.
—MATTHEW 7:12

The Golden Rule is the highest possible standard when it comes to human relations. It makes perfect sense, almost everyone is familiar with it, and virtually everyone agrees that the world would be a better place if we'd all practice it. But the truth is, we *don't* always practice it even though we want to. Why? Because it's a perfect rule, but we're imperfect people. Our flaws often get in the way. A few of them are lack of humility, lack of patience, and lack of empathy. You may recall that these are the topics covered in the first three chapters of this book. Some of us struggle with them more than others, but we're all challenged by them on occasion. And when we are, the Golden Rule slips into the background.

Here are some common examples of how each of these flaws makes it more difficult for us to live out the Golden Rule:

LACK OF HUMILITY.   A friend is telling you stories about some wonderful vacation experiences she recently had while visiting France for the first time. You've also been to France, and her stories remind you of some of the things you did while you were there. So you start talking about them, and pretty soon the conversation is about *your* experiences instead of hers. How would you feel if she had done the same thing to you?

LACK OF PATIENCE.　　You're driving in a residential area behind someone who keeps slowing down to look at house numbers. He's obviously unfamiliar with the street and is looking for a particular address. The more he slows down, the more frustrated you get because you can't go around him. So you give him a blast with the horn. How would you feel if you were the person in the other car?

LACK OF EMPATHY.　　Your spouse comes home at the end of a long day and has the need to talk about some things that happened at work. You don't find it particularly interesting, so you don't listen very attentively, and then find an excuse to go do something else. How would you feel if you came home with a need to talk, but didn't find anyone willing to listen?

I selected these three examples because they're common, and because I've been guilty of each of them. The Golden Rule is easy to quote and easy to agree with, but not always easy to practice. We too often forget to put ourselves in the place of the other person. That's because humility, patience, and empathy are difficult virtues to develop. But it's worth the effort because it results in kinder hearts and better skills in dealing with others. They're choices that can change our lives as well as the lives of people around us. The Golden Rule is still Golden.

Two of the main reasons the Golden Rule isn't practiced as consistently as it was forty years ago are major changes in society. One is the dizzying pace at which we now seem to live. There's an emphasis on speed and multitasking—get more things done in less time. And both at work and at home we want high-speed access to everything. The other major change has been a general decline in civility and manners over the past several years. It's the result of both the rapid pace of life and the proliferation of media messages that encourage us to focus on ourselves first. We get caught up in all of this, and the Golden Rule begins to fade. More than twenty years ago, Henry C. Rogers, then one of the leading public relations experts in the country, said, "If manners were an animal, it would be an endangered species."

It's important to remember that one person with good manners and good human relations skills can still make a difference. What's going on around is no reason to lower our standards of excellence in this important area. The key is maintaining control over our own lives. Dr. Thomas Lickona, one of the pioneers of the character education movement, says, "We need to be in control of ourselves—our appetites, our passions—to do right by others."

3. Work Ethic

> *If a man is called to be a street sweeper, he should sweep streets*
> *even as Michelangelo painted, or Beethoven composed music, or*
> *Shakespeare wrote poetry. He should sweep streets so well that*
> *all the hosts of heaven and earth will pause to say, "Here lived a*
> *great street sweeper who did his job well."*
>
> —MARTIN LUTHER KING, JR.

Now that you've read the beautiful statement above, go back and read a slightly different version of it. Take out the phrase "street sweeper" and replace it with the position you're currently in. Instead of "sweep streets" write in what it is that you do. It doesn't make any difference whether you're a student, pastor, salesman, stay-at-home parent, sportswriter, chef, office worker, teacher,

CEO, professional athlete, gardener, or anything else. The question is, do you maintain a high standard? Do you strive for excellence? Do you always give the best you have?

One of the nice things about growing up in the 1950s was that the messages we got were clear and straightforward. One of those messages was: If you want to be good at anything you better plan on working hard at it. It was taught and modeled in my home, it was reinforced at school and on the athletic field, and it was honored in the media. The message was that there was no short cut, no "quick and easy" way, no secret, and no magic formula for success. There was just hard work. Sadly, over the years the message has changed. Many of our young people are led to believe that there *is* a quicker and easier way—be come a star on *American Idol,* buy a lottery ticket, invest in a hot stock, get drafted out of high school by the pros. But the truth remains—there's no substitute for hard work.

Let's go back to the question I always asked my students: "Why would you ever want to give less than the best you have?" If you're at school, why not your best? If you're at work, why not your best? If you're competing in sports, why not your best? The benefits are many. Hard work builds character, leads to achievement, earns the respect of others, adds meaning to our lives, makes us feel better about ourselves, helps us develop good habits, and leads to healthier, happier, and longer lives.

4. Personal Growth and Development

> *I know of no more encouraging fact than the unquestionable*
> *ability of man to elevate his life by conscious endeavor.*
> —HENRY DAVID THOREAU

One of the most enjoyable questions I ever asked my students was a simple one: "What are the best things about life?" It was enjoyable because we had so much fun answering it. The question was not part of a master plan. It was actually the result of something going on in class one day that started out negative.

My students were in one of those collective moods—they were whining and moaning (school conditions them to do this) about how bad they had it, about how unfair things were, about how hard life was, about school, and just about everything else. "You poor things." I said (smiling). "You have it so tough. Isn't it sad that we live in a world in which the negatives so outweigh the positives."

That got their attention. Someone then said, "That's not really true." I said, "I know it's not true. I'm just trying to get you to realize it." I then explained one of my many theories on life: The more we have and the easier we have it, the more we complain. Some agreed with me; some didn't. I also said that complaining was a waste of time and energy. It poisons the atmosphere and drags other people down. I wondered aloud why they didn't talk about the good things. I asked, "What are the best things about life?" The mood in the room changed dramatically as the students came up with with several great answers. In the process, one of them asked me what *I* thought was the best thing about life. I didn't hesitate for a second. I answered, "Every day we wake up with an opportunity to become a better person than we were yesterday."

Several years earlier I had suffered a shattering loss and was at the lowest point of my life. At the urging of friends I reluctantly went to counseling. It helped more than I thought possible. The counseling was supplemented by the reading of some outstanding books. I discovered the optimistic psychology of Abraham Maslow, the spirituality of Thomas Merton, and the philosophy of Viktor Frankl, the author of *Man's Search for Meaning*. It was that book, more than anything at the time, that changed my outlook on life. As the fragmented pieces of my life came back together, I began to look forward to each new day as I had never done before. Personal growth, which had never been my thing, had become both important and exhilarating. I'm aware that one can go overboard on the personal growth thing (and I did for a while), but knowing that I have the opportunity to improve myself in some way every day still excites me.

BUILDING ON STRENGTHS; IMPROVING ON FLAWS

I want to share another activity that I did with both my high school and adult students. They always ranked it as among the best in terms of personal and lasting value. It was remarkably simple. They were to ask six people whom they knew well to give them some personal feedback on a simple form. It had the person's name on it and three spaces under this heading "Strengths." The evaluator was to write down what he or she saw as the student's best personal qualities. It also had three spaces under the word "Flaws." The evaluator was to write down areas in which he or she thought the student could improve.

We always had a lengthy discussion about this before they went out and picked their six people. I asked them if there was anyone in the room without any flaws. No hands ever went up except when a few students did it as a joke. It was important to remind them that we all have flaws. Some we're aware of; some we're not. And if we're not willing to look at them in the light of people who know us well and care about us, we'll never improve upon them. I told them they might learn a few things about themselves that could sting a little bit, but if they had the courage to face up to their flaws, they'd become better persons for it. They were encouraged to have a good, long talk with each person who filled out the form. It was important to receive thorough explanations.

If done in the right spirit, this can be an invaluable opportunity for self-examination and personal growth. I vividly recall the first time I did this activity with my students. To get a full sense of what they were experiencing, I had six people fill out forms on me also. The results were eye-opening, to say the least. Three of my colleagues pointed out an identical flaw of which I had been unaware. My discussions with them afterward helped me understand their perceptions more clearly, and I set out to make the necessary changes. Yes, it was a little uncomfortable and humbling, but it was a valuable wake-up call and a wonderful opportunity to become a better person.

> *Our prayers are answered not when we are given what we ask,*
> *but when we are challenged to be what we can be.*
>
> —MORRIS ADLER

Chapter Eleven

MISSION

LIFE IS RICHER WITH MEANING AND
PURPOSE. HAVE A CAUSE GREATER
THAN YOURSELF.

DEFINITIONS

*Mission: a specific task with which a person or a group is
charged; calling.*

—MERRIAM-WEBSTER

*Your personal mission in life is all your roles and values
distilled into a sentence or two that describe what you want to
be and accomplish in your life.*

—HYRUM W. SMITH

RELATED WORDS/ VIRTUES	OPPOSITE WORDS/ FLAWS
Vision	Emptiness
Passion	Aimlessness
Fulfillment	Cluelessness

11. Mission

More than once you have heard me say that life is a mission most of us are trying to fly without any flight plan because they never gave us one in school.

—OG MANDINO

What's the first thing that pops into your mind when you look at the question above? Would you be able to answer it without hesitation or would you need some time to think about it? It's a question I've asked of literally thousands of people of all ages for more than twenty-five years. I've asked it of groups and I've asked it of individuals. The question throws most people off. More than ninety percent of them need time to think about it and still don't come up with an answer. Here's how the dialogue usually goes when I ask it of an individual:

Question: "What's your mission in life?"
Answer: "Huh?"
Question: "What's your mission in life?"
Answer: "What do you mean?"
Question: "What's your reason for being here?"
Answer: "I'm not sure I know how to answer that."

Of the responses I received from the small percentage of people who answer immediately, these are the most common, in order of frequency:

"To be happy."
"To be rich."
"To be rich and happy."
"To take care of my family."
"To become a good [career position]."
"To retire early with a nice nest egg."
"To honor and serve God in all that I do."
"To make the world a better place."
"To be the best person I can be."
"To experience life to the fullest."

One of the best things about asking this question is that, no matter how people respond, it always leaves them thinking. Nothing is more pleasing to a teacher. I hope the question has the same effect on every person who reads this book because it's the most important one we'll ever answer. Some people equate it with the most famous question of all: What is the meaning of life? It *is* similar. Maybe another way of asking it is, "What's the meaning of *your* life?" No matter what answer you come up with, I guarantee that it will cause you to think more about what you're doing and what your purpose is.

One of the reasons I've been asking the question for so long is that it was asked of me about twenty-five years ago. And it was life-changing. I didn't have an answer at the time, but realized that I needed one. And both the question and my eventual answer have stuck in the forefront of my brain ever since. If you've never answered the question, I urge you, with every fiber of my being, to do so. It will make a huge difference in your life.

I was asked the question at a men's weekend retreat in the early 1980s. It was aptly called "Purpose Leads to Meaning; Meaning Leads to Joy." The retreat leader opened the weekend with these words: "Why are you here?" He told us that if we didn't have a good answer to his question, he was going to help us find one before the weekend was over. Not only would we find an answer, we would put it in writing in the form of a personal mission statement that would guide us for the rest of our lives. It was the most enlightening and enriching weekend any of us had ever experienced.

PURPOSE AND VALUES: WHAT'S MOST IMPORTANT TO YOU?

Our governing values lie at the very center of who we are.
—HYRUM W. SMITH

A strong set of core values leads life from the inside out . . . Your purpose is intertwined with your vision and values.
—JIM CLEMMER

Here's another question that I've asked thousands of times of my students and of people in my workshops. It comes in three parts. The first is the general question, "What's most important to you?" The second is, "List ten things, in any order, that are important to you." And finally, "Put those ten things in order of importance." What would be on your list? I strongly urge you to do this when you're finished reading this chapter. It sounds like a simple exercise, but it isn't. Some people take hours, and some take days, to get their final list in order. But all agree that it's time well spent. A few years ago one of my adult students expressed the feelings of many when he said, "I thought long and hard about this little exercise. When I finally finished, I not only felt a sense of clarity, I made a commitment to do a better job of living according to my principles. It's made a real difference."

There are two additional parts to this exercise that further help people get in touch with the relationship between what they say is important and their daily behavior. One is to list the ten activities, other than sleep, that occupy most of your time. After listing the ten, they put them in order of time spent on each. We often find inconsistencies when we look at the list of ten things we claim to be most important and the other list of the ten activities that occupy most of our time. Example: Some men don't even put golf on their top-ten-values list, but it ranks pretty high on the time-spent list.

The other part of the exercise is to write a sentence after each word on the value list. In it briefly explain what you *do* each day that proves it's important to you. Example: Many people list God and family as their top two priorities. But they often struggle when asked how they prove it by their daily actions. The point is that it's much easier to say something is important to us than it is to practice what we preach. That's why people say these exercises are so helpful them. The pace of life and our many responsibilities often cause us to lose focus. These exercises have a way of getting us to refocus and bring an increased sense of order to our lives. Several of my students have told me they put their top-ten values list somewhere visible so they can look at it every day to help them stay on track.

Doing these simple exercises helps people in a number of ways. First, many become aware for the first time that they even *have* a set of governing values, and that these values direct their behavior. Second, some people discover that they've unknowingly acquired a few negative values, ones that ultimately lead to pain. This discovery leads them to either alter or eliminate them. Third, this entire process of identifying, clarifying, and reordering their value systems seems to rejuvenate them. A number of people say these exercises not only helped them get back on track, but gave them an increased sense of power over their lives.

PURPOSE AND THE PARADOX OF LIFE

*Many people have a wrong idea of what constitutes true
happiness. It is not attained through self-gratification, but
through fidelity to a worthy purpose.*

—HELEN KELLER

*Service is the rent we pay to be living. It is the very purpose of
life and not something you do in your spare time.*

—MARIAN WRIGHT EDELMAN

Merriam-Webster defines paradox as "a statement that is seemingly contradictory or opposed to common sense and yet is perhaps true." Here's the paradox that most often prevents people from finding their purpose in life:

THE HUMAN CONDITION. As explained in the first chapter on humility, we come into the world thinking we're the center of it. Everything revolves around us, and other people are here for the sole purpose of taking care of our needs and making us happy. Our own purpose in life seems to be pleasure—having fun and acquiring things. In addition, we're constantly bombarded with messages that reinforce this mentality: "Take care of yourself first," "You deserve it," "You're worth it." Is it any wonder that so many people never grow beyond this "me first" approach to life?

THE PARADOX. The more we follow the selfish inclinations of our human nature, the more we seek self-gratification, the more we come up empty. All those things that the world tells us we should be constantly seeking—pleasure, fun, luxury, power, status—never lead to true joy and fulfillment. Life actually works in the opposite manner. We find real joy and fulfillment, not in getting, but in giving; not in being served, but in service; and not in taking, but in contributing. Learning to overcome our selfish nature is one of the hardest lessons of life. It's also one of our greatest and most constant challenges. But we need to learn the lesson and meet the challenge if we want to know what it feels like to be fully human and to know that our lives matter for something other than pleasing ourselves. The real paradox is that our rewards in life will always be in direct proportion to what we contribute to life.

I don't want to imply here that we have to deny ourselves all the material pleasures of the world. It's not wrong to earn a good salary, have a nice home and car, or vacation in beautiful places. These are some of the rewards of hard work and self-discipline, and we have every right to enjoy them. We can do this and still find many ways to be of service to others and make the world a better place. It's not a matter of choosing one over the other. We're not all called to be Mahatma Gandhi or Mother Teresa. But we *are* all called to serve.

At the beginning of this section I used quotes by Helen Keller and Marian Wright Edelman to illuminate the connection between purpose in life and service to others. A library search on these two related topics uncovered several additional comments by well-known and highly respected people throughout history. Rather than try to paraphrase them, I'll let them speak in their own wisdom:

A generous heart, kind speech, and a life of service and compassion are the things which renew humanity.

—BUDDHA

I know of no great men except those who have rendered great service to the human race.

—VOLTAIRE

No man has ever risen to the real stature of spiritual manhood until he has found that it is finer to serve somebody else than it is to serve himself.

—WOODROW WILSON

Consciously or unconsciously, every one of us does render some service or other. If we cultivate the habit of doing this service deliberately, our desire for service will steadily grow stronger, and will make, not only our own happiness, but that of the world at large.

—MAHATMA GANDHI

The highest destiny of the individual is to serve rather than to rule.

—ALBERT EINSTEIN

Everyone can be great because anyone can serve. You don't have to have a college degree to serve. You don't even have to make your subject and your verb agree to serve. . . . You only need a heart full of grace.

—MARTIN LUTHER KING, JR.

You can get everything in life you want, if you help enough other people get what they want.

—ZIG ZIGLAR

The more you serve others, the more fulfilled your life will be.

—DR. BERNIE SIEGEL

DISCOVERING YOUR PURPOSE

Everyone has a purpose in life beyond one's immediate interests and gratifications, though that purpose frequently goes undiscovered.

—JOHN MARKS TEMPLETON

Maybe you've already discovered your mission or purpose. If you have, then you understand how much more meaningful life can be, and reading this only reinforces what you already know. If this is the case, I would encourage you to look for opportunities to help others find their mission in life. It's one of the greatest contributions you'll ever make. You don't have to be a classroom teacher like I was to ask the questions that are explained at the beginning of this chapter. They can be asked in your family, at work, in your place of worship, or with friends. You're likely to make a positive and lasting impact on someone you care about.

One of the most important turning points of my own life occurred when a dear friend and teacher helped me rediscover my mission in life. I had known since the ninth grade that I wanted to be a teacher. But as I was about to graduate from college, I kept hearing about how little money teachers made and how little prestige they had. Some of my friends who were going to law school knew that I had a logical mind and was a conscientious and hardworking student. They convinced me that I would make the perfect lawyer, would make way more money, and would be in a position of greater stature. After a lot of thinking, I applied to law school. I was accepted and was also awarded an academic scholarship. It seemed like the right decision.

Law school was stimulating. The professors were excellent and the subject matter was interesting, often fascinating. It was mostly common sense and logic, with a lot of hard work. All of this was fine with me, and I was doing well academically, so my decision to go to law school was confirmed as the right one. But about halfway through the year, I began to have some doubts. I couldn't quite picture myself in a law office or in a courtroom arguing about how much someone's injury or breach of contract was worth. The more I thought about it, the blurrier the picture became.

I needed to talk to someone older and wiser who also knew me well. I went to see Father Edmund Smyth, one of my former history professors and the dean of the college of arts and science. Among Father Smyth's many admirable qualities were insight, empathy, and the ability to give sound advice, which he had done several times during my years as an undergraduate. I told him I was having a hard time seeing myself as a lawyer and wondered out loud if needing a picture was stupid. He said, "It's not stupid at all. We all need pictures to help us find our way." He then asked me, "What *can* you picture yourself doing?" I answered in one word: "Teaching." He smiled and said, "I knew that. I think you just needed to verbalize it to someone else."

Later that day I withdrew from law school and applied for acceptance into the teacher-training program. Ever since that day more than forty years ago, teaching has been my profession, a big part of my mission in life, and my passion. It has given me more purpose, meaning, and joy than I could have ever expected, and more than I could even begin to explain. I was blessed to find my calling and I was blessed to have a friend and mentor like Father Smyth to help me "see" my mission and get back on the right track.

Obviously, everyone's story is different. We find our mission in life in many different ways, but there are a few principles in my story that are universal, and which might be helpful to those still looking for a purpose. The "picture" is more important than it probably sounds. Our mental images act like magnets that pull us in the direction of our calling. The clearer they are, the more we're able to see ourselves doing what we were meant to do. Having a mentor, or mentors, is also important. It's invaluable to get the perspective of another person, especially a wise one who knows us well. And it's important to realize that what we enjoy the most is a big part of our mission in life. We serve others better when we like what we're doing. For example, I always loved school—elementary, high school, and college—so it made sense for me to turn school into both my career and my mission in life.

I was fortunate that my career and a major part of my mission in life merged into one. That's not the case for everyone. Sometimes your profession is also your mission in life, but often it isn't. Teachers, pastors, counselors, social workers, and health professionals are good examples of people who fulfill their mission of serving others while doing their jobs. But there are many other people who see their jobs as separate from their mission. For example, I have four friends who work in the grocery business, the financial sector, construction, and sales. They enjoy their jobs and do them well but don't consider them to be part of their mission in life, which is serving others. One of them is devoted to working with Catholic Charities, another serves God through a variety of positions in his church, another devotes thousands of hours to youth sports and coaching, and one does volunteer work in schools, especially in mentoring. They all help other people in their jobs, but their real mission is in improving their communities while serving others in outside pursuits.

Purpose defines our contribution to life. It may find expression through family, community, relationship, work, and spiritual activities. We receive from life what we give, and in the process we understand more of what it means to discover our purpose.

—RICHARD J. LEIDER

Here are some fairly simple suggestions for finding your mission or helping others find theirs. Write out specific responses to the following:

1. What is your mission in life?
2. Make a list of your top ten values in order of importance.
3. With the help of people who know you well, make a list of your best personal qualities and talents.
4. Which of these qualities and talents can best be used to enrich the lives of others?
5. How much time per week do you spend in making the world a better place?
6. What do you see as an important need in your community?
7. What's the best way you can contribute to meeting that need?

FINDING MEANING AND JOY IN A MIGHTY PURPOSE

This is the true joy in life, the being used for a purpose recognized by yourself as a mighty one; the being thoroughly worn out before you are thrown on the scrap heap. . .

—GEORGE BERNARD SHAW

The most joyful people in the world are the ones who've found that mighty purpose mentioned above by George Bernard Shaw. The reasons are neither complicated nor deeply philosophical or theological. They're actually quite simple, because they're based on a simple law of life that's been mentioned several times already in this book. And because teachers love to reinforce (repeat) their main points, here it is again:

> OUR REWARDS IN LIFE WILL ALWAYS BE
> IN DIRECT PROPORTION TO WHAT WE
> CONTRIBUTE TO LIFE.

To many people, this is one of those sayings that has a nice ring to it, but they think it doesn't apply to everyone—only to people like Schweitzer and Gandhi and Dr. King and Mother Teresa. They're wrong. It applies to *every* person on the face of the earth. There are other people who simply don't believe it. Their philosophy of life is "Me, Me, Me." And that's why they're empty, lonely, and unhappy most of the time. There are still others who believe this simple law of life, but think it applies only after they've had their fun. They have it backward. Fun isn't the main course of life. It's the dessert. The main course is meaningful work and service to others. And the joy that comes from them is better than fun.

So what might this "mighty purpose" be? Amnesty International? The Red Cross? The Salvation Army? Habitat for Humanity? The Sierra Club? The Humane Society? The Billy Graham Crusade? Big Brothers and Sisters? The NAACP? St. Vincent de Paul? City of Hope? Alcoholics Anonymous? The American Jewish Committe? The Blood Bank? It could be one of these wonderful organizations or it could be one of the lesser-known organizations that exist for the same reasons: to help others and to make the world a better place.

But it doesn't have to be one of these, or *any* organization, for that matter. As George Bernard Shaw directs us in the quote at the beginning of this section, I can assure you that there are mighty purposes all around you. Your first responsibility is to recognize them. Your second responsibility is to find the one that's most suited to your personality and talents. It could be a local school, a youth program, your place of worship, community service, a homeless shelter, or something of your own invention. The needs are there. Your third responsibility is to serve in the best way you can. An increase in meaning and joy will follow naturally.

YOUR MISSION IN WRITING

A personal mission statement addresses three questions:
1) What is my life about?   2) What do I stand for?
3) What action am I taking to live what my life is about
and what I stand for?
A useful mission statement should include two pieces: what you
wish to accomplish and contribute, and who you want to be—
the character strengths and qualities you wish to develop.
                                        —KATHARINE HANSEN

There have been three times in my life when I was asked to write something down and found the result life-changing. The first time was near the end of eighth grade, when Sister Anne, my teacher, asked us to write ten lifetime goals. We wrote things like "be happy," "make lots of money," and "be famous." She accepted none of them, and then taught us to write specific, achievable goals. She also encouraged us to continue writing goals for the rest of our lives. I loved Sister Anne and always did what she asked. So I've been writing goals for more than fifty years now—literally thousands of them! Few things can make life more rewarding or enjoyable than working on and achieving personal goals. In fact, the best definition of success I've ever seen is Earl Nightingale's: "Success is the progressive accomplishment of worthy goals." The second time I wrote down something that was life-changing was in a workshop early in my teaching career when I was in my mid-twenties. I wrote down the same thing I asked you to write down earlier in this chapter—the ten things that are most important to you, in their proper order. At the time I didn't take it too seriously. It was during a teacher staff development day, and what we did on those days was usually a waste of time. But this exercise wouldn't leave my mind, so I spent a long time later on my own getting those values in order. The workshop leader told us that our values might change, and that we should look at and revise our list regularly. I didn't like him as much as I liked Sister Anne, but I knew in my heart that if this exercise was going to be meaningful, I needed to do some follow-up work, just as I did with my goals. Looking at and clarifying our values—and living by them regularly—is even more important than writing goals.

The third time I wrote something down that was life-changing was when I wrote my personal mission statement at that men's retreat when I was in my early forties. It has kept me focused for almost twenty-five years. I keep it at the top of the first page in my journal. Right below it I have some powerful quotes from wise people that reinforce my purpose in life. The mission statement and the quotes are the first things I look at each morning, whether I'm at home or on the road. They've been changed a little over the years, but the core remains the same. I can't imagine going through even one day without looking at these thing first.

Although I did these exercises separately and years apart, it finally dawned on me how closely related they are. Our values, our goals, and our mission in life can't really be separated. Together, they form a triangle for a meaningful and joyful life.

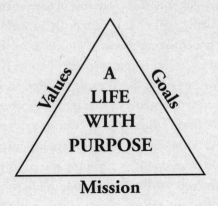

If the concept of a personal mission statement is new to you, it's important to understand that there's no set formula and no set length. The definition by Katharine Hansen at the beginning of this section was the best I could find. It provides an excellent starting place. The book I would most recommend on this topic is *What Matters Most: The Power of Living Your Values,* by Hyrum W. Smith. He thoroughly explains the concepts of "governing values" and personal mission statements, and provides several practical examples. One of the most valuable things you'll ever do is write your own personal mission statement, and then look at it and live by it for the rest of your life. It will lead to unexpected rewards.

When you heed the calling of your heart, you are following your purpose. Having purpose in your life gives you the courage to do the things you are meant to do.

—RHONDA BRITTEN

Chapter Twelve

SCRIPTURE

THE SCRIPTURES ARE A SOURCE OF
STRENGTH AND COMFORT. USE
THEM TO ENRICH YOUR LIFE.

DEFINITIONS

Scripture: a body of writings considered sacred or authoritative; the books of the Bible; a passage from the Bible.

—MERRIAM-WEBSTER

Take all of this Book that you can by reason, and the balance by faith, and you will live and die a better man.

—ABRAHAM LINCOLN

RELATED WORDS/ VIRTUES	OPPOSITE WORDS/ FLAWS
Holy Book	Horoscope
Old Testament	Astrology
New Testament	Psychics

12. Scripture

ON MATTERS OF FAITH AND COMPASSION

*We have just enough religion to make us hate, but not enough
to make us love one another.*

—JONATHAN SWIFT

Let your religion be less of a theory and more of a love affair.

—G. K. CHESTERTON

This and the following chapter on prayer are the most challenging to write simply because they both deal with matters of faith. We have a wide variety of beliefs when it comes to spiritual matters, and I respect all of them. I don't want to tell my readers what they should believe any more than I want to tell them how they should live. But I have a strong need to be true to myself. The scriptures and prayer are essential parts of my own purpose, meaning, and joy, and I would feel I had copped out if I didn't include them. The trick is being able to write about them in such a way that both the people who share my Christian faith and those who don't might benefit.

Please keep in mind that the word "Christian" can conjure up many different notions. In politics we run the gamut from super-conservative right-wing, close-minded fanatics to ultraliberal left-wing, close-minded fanatics. Sadly, the same spectrum exists within Christianity. There are some pretty strange things done in the name of religion when they come from either of those extremist positions. And quite frankly, they cause me both pain and embarrassment. We're admonished in several places in the Bible not to judge others, but it's done regularly in some Christian churches. If ever there was a person who showed compassion to those who were different, it was Jesus. Yet, many of those who claim to follow him don't seem to see that as part of the program.

Fortunately, the overwhelming majority of Christians, the ones who *don't* get all the publicity, are more moderate in their beliefs, and they work hard at applying the principles of their faith to everyday living. They are a joy to be around, as are people of other faiths who peaceably live out their convictions without harming or judging others. There are some universal elements in the teaching of all religions—kindness, compassion, honesty, caring, giving, and respect for creation. I want to be among these people of faith who live by their governing values, and hope my words in these two chapters will be both informative and enlightening.

One of the most rewarding professional experiences I ever had was teaching a course called World Religions to adults at the University of San Francisco. What made it so exciting was that many of my students had very limited knowledge regarding spiritual matters. Many didn't know the Old Testament from the New, didn't know what the Golden Rule was, didn't know the Ten Commandments and didn't know where to find them, didn't know what a Christian was and didn't know the difference between a Catholic, a Protestant, and a Mormon. But they were open to all of it, and many felt that it was one of the most valuable courses they had ever taken. They found it enlightening to finally grasp some basic terminology pertaining to faith, to understand the core beliefs of the major religions, and to see the similarities among them. Many of them voiced the opinion that we'd have more religious tolerance if a similar course was taught in every elementary and high school, both public and private.

One of the things that made teaching the course so pleasant was the book we used. It's called *The World's Religions,* written by

Huston Smith. It's a fair and balanced look at the history and basic beliefs of several of the world's religions. It's also easy to read and understand. I highly recommend it if you're interested in increasing your knowledge in this important area of life.

> *A friendly study of the world's religions is a sacred duty.*
> —MAHATMA GANDHI

For many years one of my favorite authors has been Rabbi Harold Kushner. I've read all of his books, some of them more than once. He has a special ability to write about life and meaning and spirituality in a way that touches a person of any faith or no faith. He brings new life to stories from the Old Testament that are meaningful and enriching to all of us. I hope to do the same with some examples from both the Old and New Testaments. Here is a good example from Kushner's book *When All You Ever Wanted Isn't Enough.*

> *It matters if we learn how to share our lives with others,*
> *making them and their world different, rather than try to*
> *hoard life for ourselves. It matters if we learn to recognize the*
> *pleasures of every day, food and work and love and friendship,*
> *as encounters with the divine, encounters that teach us not only*
> *that God is real but that we are real too. Those things make all*
> *the difference.*
> —RABBI HAROLD KUSHNER

UNDERSTANDING AND APPLYING THE BIBLE

> *Most people are bothered by those passages of Scripture they do*
> *not understand, but the passages that bother me are those I do*
> *understand.*
> —MARK TWAIN

"The Bible is too confusing," is a comment I've heard countless times. I've also heard that it's too long and has too much sex and violence in it. The truth is that parts of the Bible *are* difficult to understand. The Old Testament is long and often confusing. It's part history, part prophecy, and part poetry. But it's worth exploring, even if you know you'll never understand it all. There are some good books available that simplify it. Two of the best are *30 Days to Understanding the Bible,* by Max E. Anders, and *What the Bible is All About,* by Dr. Henrietta Mears. Both of these books have been highly recommended for years, and each has been updated several times. They cover both the Old and New Testaments. In addition, many churches and synagogues offer excellent courses that help beginners understand the basics. The Old Testament is critically important because it's the foundation for many of the world's leading religions.

The best thing about the Bible is that both the Old and New Testaments can be studied for a lifetime, and each time we do it, we can be inspired in a new and refreshing way. It's possible to read a passage more than forty times, then on the forty-first, a light goes on. And while there will always be parts that are either open to interpretation or confusing, there are many more which speak directly to us. A good example is, "Treat other people exactly as you would like to be treated by them—this is the essence of all true religions" (Matthew 7:12. Phillips trans.). Commonly known as the Golden Rule, it's much easier to say than it is to do consistently. This and other passages that tell us to not judge, to love one another, and to forgive must be the ones Mark Twain was referring to in his quote above. They call us to be humble, patient, compassionate, kind, and forgiving while the world often tells us to be selfish. None of these great biblical virtues are easy to acquire, but they are well worth the struggle.

I never owned a Bible until I was thirty-one years old. My first one was a leather-bound copy of the J. B. Phillips translation of the New Testament that was given to me as a gift by Tim Hansel, one of my dearest friends. I was not a Christian at the time. In fact, I was in a post-divorce and anti-God state, so the Bible made for an interesting gift. My first inclination was to put it on a shelf where it would look nice, but not read it. I was heavily into "human potential" psychology at the time, and was doing extensive reading about the theories of Abraham Maslow, Carl Rogers, Fritz Perls, Eric Berne, and several other leaders in the field. My goal was to be "self-actualized," whatever that meant, and "fully human," whatever that meant.

But Tim was a special friend, and he had touched my life in a way that no one else ever had. He was also one of the most joyful and affirming persons I'd ever known. He had an extraordinary gift for enhancing the lives of those around him, and for bringing out the best in them. I owed it to him and to our friendship to open that Bible. I was in for one of the biggest surprises of my life!

Only a few pages into the Gospel of Matthew, Jesus tells his followers, "You must change your hearts." That got my attention because my heart was in a bad place at the time—a negative, angry, and resentful place. Then I got to the next page and Jesus talked about humility, kindness, honesty, goodness, mercy, and peace. That sounded pretty "fully human" to me, and it dawned on me that it had been preached and written almost two thousand years before the "human potential" movement came along.

At the end of this section known as "The Sermon on the Mount" and as the "Beatitudes," Jesus says, "You are the world's light—it is impossible to hide a town built on top of a hill. Men do not light a lamp and put it under a bucket. They put it on a lamp-stand and it gives light for everybody in the house. Let your light shine like that in the sight of men" (Matthew 5:14–16). This immediately made me think of Tim. He was a very bright light who helped me see things differently.

But I was both slow and stubborn. I finished reading the New Testament, highlighting, underlining in different colors, and writing in the margins. But I also stayed with my "human potential" reading for several more years. I figured I could have the best of both worlds—psychology *and* the wisdom from the Bible—without making any kind of religious commitment. And I could still sleep in on Sundays. But it was a lot like eating Chinese food. I'd get full and feel "self-actualized" for a short time, then feel totally empty for several days. This was getting tiresome. God seemed to be calling . . . and calling . . . and calling. He finally got through, and at age thirty-nine I answered. Basically, I was saying, "I don't really like this emptiness, and my psychology books don't seem to be helping over the long haul. Do you have a better plan?" He did. He said, "Come to me, all of you who are weary and overburdened, and I will give you rest!" (Matthew 11:28). I couldn't believe how much better living had become.

> *All scripture is inspired by God and is useful for teaching the*
> *faith and correcting error, for re-setting the direction of a man's*
> *life and training him in good living.*
>
> —II TIMOTHY 3:16

I found rest. I also found a huge increase in both purpose and meaning in my life. And to make it even better, I found more joy than I had thought possible. That's the very reason C. S. Lewis wrote a book called *Surprised by Joy.* He was a great intellect who'd been an avowed atheist for many years, and at the request of several of his contemporaries, he explained the almost torturous process of his conversion. His biggest surprise was joy.

None of this means that being a person of faith is easy. There's absolutely nothing easy about it. "Your spirit is willing, but human nature is weak" (Matthew 26:41).

> *Here, then, is the real problem of our negligence. We fail in our duty to study God's Word not so much because it is difficult to understand, not so much because it is dull and boring, but because it is work. Our problem is not a lack of intelligence or a lack of passion. Our problem is that we are lazy.*
>
> —R. C. SPROUL

Few things in life are more difficult than practicing humility, patience, empathy, giving, and forgiving. Those just happen to be the subjects of the first five chapters in this book. They're also the subjects of countless verses in the Bible, in both the Old and New Testaments. God calls us to live these and other virtues in spite of our weak human nature. We're back to the paradox of life I explained in an earlier chapter—the more selfless we become, the more rewards we find. But it will never be easy.

THE SCRIPTURES AND OUR NEED TO BE GOOD

There are a few times in each of our lives in which we have an epiphany. We see something that's been around for a long time and it suddenly becomes crystal clear. I had one of those in 1986 when I was reading the book by Rabbi Kushner that was mentioned earlier, *When All You Ever Wanted Isn't Enough*. All of us know that we're supposed to be "good," and we've been given all kinds of reasons. It's our duty, it will make the world a better place, our parents and teachers want us to be good, we'll get in trouble if we don't, and we'll be rewarded if we do. Rabbi Kushner gives us an even better reason—we *need* to be good.

> *Human beings have a need to be good. . . . Our human nature*
> *is such that we need to be helpful, thoughtful, and generous as*
> *much as we need to eat, sleep, and exercise. When we eat too*
> *much and exercise too little, we feel out of sorts. Even our*
> *personalities are affected. And when we are selfish and deceitful,*
> *it has the same effect. We become out of touch with our real*
> *selves; we forget what it feels like to feel good.*
>
> —RABBI HAROLD KUSHNER

I think the heart of the message in the Scriptures, both Old and New Testaments, is to be good. There are two main reasons. The first is that God asks us to, and it pleases Him when we choose to obey. Second, it makes life here on earth a whole lot better, both for others and for ourselves. You don't have to be a biblical scholar to see that this common thread runs throughout the Scriptures, beginning with the first chapter of the Book of Genesis in the Old Testament—"So God created man in his own image" (1:27)—and ending with the last chapter of the Book of Revelation in the New Testament: "Let the good man continue his good deeds, and the holy man continue his holiness" (22:11).

The search for the good life is as old as the human race. That's why seminars, speeches, books, videos, and tapes promising to reveal the secret to finding it rake in millions of dollars each year. I'm sorry if this disappoints you, but there's not a single secret revealed in this book or in any of my other books. In fact, I get a chuckle every time I see the word "secret" on a book. If it's a secret, why would you want to put it into a book so everyone else will know about it? It can't be a secret once you've made it available to the rest of the world. It's like my earlier comment about "self-help" books. If you're going to help yourself, why read a book written by someone else? Keep in mind, I'm not criticizing these books. Many of them have been of great value to me. It's the "self-help" label they've been given that I object to.

I promise you, the good life is available to all of us, and it's not a secret. I've been studying the real meaning of success, and its ingredients, for more than forty years. And no matter whom I read about, whom I talk to, or what I read, real success always boils down to four critical characteristics:

1. A good attitude
2. Respect and kindness
3. Hard work
4. Honesty

You can both honor God and find worldly success by choosing a good attitude, treating other people with respect and kindness, working hard, and being honest. You'll also find more purpose and meaning in your life, and you'll meet with unexpected joy. I also promise that the formula for this good life has been available in the Scriptures for thousands of years. It's never been a secret. Just don't expect it to jump out at you right away, and don't expect it to be easy to follow. I've been convinced for many years that life was never designed to be easy. The good life is not for sissies.

Here are a few things the Scriptures tell us about being successful:

ATTITUDE IN THE SCRIPTURES

I have set before you life and death, blessings and curses. Now choose life, so that you and your children may live.

—DEUTERONOMY 30:19

As a man thinketh in his heart, so is he.

—PROVERBS 23:7

Everything is possible to the man who believes.

—MARK 9:23

The carnal attitude sees no further than natural things. But the spiritual attitude reaches out after things of the spirit . . . life and inward peace.

—ROMANS 8:5–6

Fix your minds on whatever is true and honourable and just and pure and lovely and praiseworthy.

—EPHESIANS 4:8

RESPECT AND KINDNESS IN THE SCRIPTURES

Treat other people exactly as you would like to be treated by them—this is the essence of all true religion.

—MATTHEW 7:12

Thou shalt love they neighbor as thyself.

—MATTHEW 22:37

As far as your responsibility goes, live at peace with everyone.

—ROMANS 12:18

So let us concentrate on the things which make for harmony, and on the growth of one another's character.

—ROMANS 14:19

*Above everything else, be truly loving, for love is the golden
chain of all the virtues.*

—Colossians 4:14

HARD WORK IN THE SCRIPTURES

All hard work brings a profit.

—Proverbs 14:23

Whatever your hands find to do, do it with all your might.

—Ecclesiastes 2:10

Whatever you do, put your whole heart and soul into it.

—Colossians 3:23

*Live life, then, with a due sense of responsibility, not as men
who do not know the meaning of life, but as those who do.
Make the best use of your time, despite all the difficulties of
these days.*

—Ephesians 5:16–17

Know that each man's work will one day be shown for what it is.

—I Corinthians 3:13

HONESTY IN THE SCRIPTURES

You shall not steal. You shall not give false testimony.

—Exodus 20:15–16

You deserve honesty from the heart; yes, utter sincerity and truthfulness. Oh give me this wisdom.

—PSALM 51:6 (THE LIVING BIBLE)

Lies will get any man into trouble, but honesty is its own defense. Telling the truth gives a man great satisfaction, and hard work returns many blessings to him.

—PROVERBS 12:13–14

The Lord hates cheating and delights in honesty.

—PROVERBS 11:1

Be careful to do what is right in the eyes of everyone.

—ROMANS 12:17

STRENGTH, COMFORT, AND GROWTH ON A DAILY BASIS

When you read God's Word, you must constantly be saying to yourself, "It is talking to me, and about me."

—SOREN KIERKEGAARD

In *Life's Greatest Lessons* I point out that habits are the key to all success. Whether we like it or not, or even believe it or not, we are creatures of habit. Many philosophers and psychologists have gone so far as to say that we are slaves of our habits, that they rule our lives. Aristotle said, "We are what we repeatedly do." This can be good or bad, depending on our habits. The keys to success lie in changing bad habits and developing good habits.

Many years ago a dear friend and mentor told me that he started every day on a positive and uplifting note. He said when he got up in the morning, before looking at the newspaper or turning on the radio or TV, which were sure to bombard him with bad news, he spent some quiet time in his study reading the Scriptures. He said it not only got his day off to a good start, it reminded and inspired him to be the person he wanted to be.

I could partly identify with him because I was also doing some inspiring and uplifting reading the first thing every morning. The difference was in the content of what we were reading. He was reading the Scriptures, and I was reading psychology and motivational (self-help) books. My thinking at the time was that my friend was reading about religion and I was reading about behavior and the real world. A few years later I was given that copy of the New Testament, and my perception of both Scripture and "the real world" changed dramatically. This book was talking to me, and it gave me far greater reasons for improving myself as a person. I've been reading the Scriptures every morning ever since.

If you are a person of faith, I would strongly encourage you to read regularly from the holy books of your denomination. If you're a nonbeliever, I encourage you to acquaint yourself with the Scriptures and the primary holy books of other major faiths because I'm confident that you'll find the reading both enjoyable and enlightening. Keep in mind what Zig Ziglar, a man who also reads the Scriptures daily, said earlier: "You are what you are because of what goes into your mind." People who put the message of the Scriptures into their minds regularly claim the following benefits:

1. It is a great way to start every morning.
2. It strengthens and reinforces one's faith.
3. It offers comfort and peace.

4. It gets people to work on their weaknesses.
5. It helps people stay focused throughout the day.
6. It leads to personal growth—for all the right reasons.

The Bible is not an end in itself, but a means to bring men to an intimate and satisfying knowledge of God, that they may enter into Him, that they may delight in His Presence, may taste and know the inner sweetness of the very God Himself in the core and center of their hearts.

—A. W. TOZER

Chapter Thirteen

PRAYER

EVERY PRAYER IS ANSWERED. PRAY,
PRAY, PRAY!

DEFINITIONS

*Pray: to make a request in a humble manner; to address God
or a god with adoration, confession, supplication, or thanksgiving.*

—MERRIAM-WEBSTER

Prayer: the very highest energy of which the mind is capable.

—SAMUEL TAYLOR COLERIDGE

RELATED WORDS/ VIRTUES	OPPOSITE WORDS/ FLAWS
Honor	Wish
Confess	Hope
Thank	Crave

13. Prayer

DEFINING PRAYER: METHODS AND TYPES

Prayer is the affectionate reaching out of the mind for God.
—ST. AUGUSTINE

The Prayer of the Skeptic:
God, I don't know whether you exist or not, but if you do,
please show me who you are.

—PETER KREEFT

In December 2004, *U.S. News & World Report* surveyed Americans representing a variety of belief systems about their prayer habits. Of the fifty-six hundred people who responded, 64 percent claimed that they pray more than once per day. That's a lot of prayer. But prayer means different things to different people, so any discussion of it should begin with attempts not only to define it, but to understand the various methods and types. Far too many people think prayer is simply asking God for things, but it's much more than that. As the Merriam-Webster definition on the title page of this chapter points out, prayer includes, among other things, adoration, confession, supplication (asking), and thanksgiving.

People of all faiths agree that prayer is our way of communicating with God. They also agree that we can pray in any place and at any time. What they *don't* seem to agree upon is the **why** and the **how** of prayer. People have countless different reasons to pray and use a wide variety of methods. It might be helpful to examine the many ways people pray and the types of prayer that have been practiced for thousands of years.

DIFFERENT METHODS OF PRAYING

- Privately or with others
- Silently or out loud
- Talking or singing
- Dancing, clapping, lifting hands
- Sitting, standing, kneeling, lying prostrate, lying on your back
- Personal, traditional, or reciting scripture

TYPES OF PRAYER

LISTENING AND WAITING. This is the type of prayer that's used the least, and is the most difficult, but should be used the most. Since everyone agrees that prayer is communicating with God, shouldn't we be listening more than talking? So many of our prayers are yakking about what we need. What we really need is to spend more time listening to what God wants of us. Although this form of prayer is the most challenging, because the mind tends to wander while listening to God, it's also the most comforting and rewarding. God *does* speak to us. We need to learn to listen.

> *I always begin my prayer in silence. God speaks to us*
> *in the silence of our hearts.*
>
> —MOTHER TERESA

> *Prayer is exhaling the spirit of man and inhaling*
> *the spirit of God.*
>
> —EDWIN KEITH

Would we go to a doctor, rattle off our symptoms, and then get up and leave? Of course not. But that's how a lot of people pray—they talk but don't listen.

—BISHOP FULTON SHEEN

WORSHIP AND ADORATION.   This is the type of prayer that helps us stay humble. It reminds us that we're not the center of the universe, that God is. Real worship is an acknowledgment of that, a genuine expression of our love for God, and a submission to His love and will for us. Submitting and obeying are not things most of us are good at, but when they involve God, there are some incredible rewards: We become better persons, we experience a deeper sense of inner peace, and we become more joyful.

Prayer is the unfolding of one's will to God that He may fulfill it.

—ST. THOMAS AQUINAS

CONFESSION AND REPENTANCE.   This is another type of prayer that helps us work on our humility, because the truth is that we mess up every day due to our pride and self-centeredness. Two of our most common sins are judging others and gossiping, but there are plenty more ways in which we offend God. The good news is that God is very forgiving. His forgiveness begins with our confession, and continues with our dependence upon Him as a source of strength and renewal.

Then I acknowledged my sin to you and did not cover up my iniquity.
I said, "I will confess my transgressions to the Lord"—and you forgave the guilt of my sin.

—KING DAVID, PSALM 32:5

PRAISE AND THANKSGIVING. We spend a lot more time and energy complaining than we do expressing thanks. But it should be the other way around because we have far more to be thankful for than to grumble about. If we acknowledge God as the creator of the universe, then we should regularly thank him for every person, thing, and experience that has blessed our lives. Thankfulness is at the heart of faith and worship.

Praise God from whom all blessings flow.

—THOMAS KEN

PETITION AND SUPPLICATION. These are two terms often used to describe the type of prayers in which we ask for something. Sometimes we ask for "things," sometimes we ask for the strength to deal with a challenge or heartbreak, and sometimes we ask for wisdom and discernment. There's no way of knowing what percentage of prayer involves our asking for something, but it's believed to be high. People often turn to God when they need help, and can't find it anywhere else. This type of prayer is consistent with God's teaching.

Be anxious for nothing, but in everything by prayer
and supplication, with thanksgiving, let your requests
be made known to God.

—PHILIPPIANS 4:6

INTERCESSION FOR SELF AND OTHERS. This means to intercede or plead on behalf of others. We're either praying for someone else or asking others to pray for us. It's a common form of prayer in many faiths. Sometimes people are too weak or dispirited to pray for themselves, so they ask for help from others.

Leaders in many places of worship frequently call among members to pray for others in the congregation and to pray together for a variety of causes.

> *First, supplications, prayers, intercessions and thanksgiving*
> *should be made on behalf of all men.*
>   —1 TIMOTHY 2:1

DEALING WITH THE DEVIL.   Call it anything you want— Satan, the Devil, forces of evil, powers of darkness—there's something bad out there that seems to want a piece of us. Not one person in the history of the human race has escaped the temptation to do something he or she knows is wrong. In fact, most of us are tempted daily. It's part of the human condition. Resisting evil is one of the main reasons we're encouraged to pray regularly.

> *Put on God's complete armor so that you can successfully resist*
> *all the devil's methods of attack.*
>   —EPHESIANS 6:11

THREE COMMON MISTAKES

O ne of my goals in writing this chapter is to show that prayer involves much more than asking God for things. I hope I've been able to do that thus far. But I need to warn you: The most difficult aspects of prayer are yet to come. Here are three of the most common mistakes people make regarding prayer:

1. THEY TREAT GOD AS IF HE'S A GENIE IN A BOTTLE. They make a wish, and if it isn't granted, they think they got a bad bottle or a lazy genie. So they give up. There's a big difference between wishing (hoping, fantasizing, dreaming) and praying. Prayer is seeking God's will, not our own.

2. THEY PLAY "LET'S MAKE A DEAL" WITH GOD.

When I was in high school, some of my most fervent and personal prayers came at the free throw line near the end of a close basketball game. The prayer usually went some thing like this: "God, if you help me make this free throw, I won't think about sex for a week." I know I made most of those free throws, but can't seem to remember how well I did on my part of the bargain. There are many versions of this type of prayer, as almost everyone has a story. Most of us eventually learn that God is not a game show.

3. THEY INSULT GOD BY ASKING FOR SILLY THINGS.

My free throws are a good example. God couldn't care less whether I made them or not or who won the game. And that goes for *all* sports. God has more important things to be concerned about. And I'm pretty sure he's not too concerned about our dream cars, our jewelry wishes, or our lottery tickets. What God *is* interested in is helping us become the types of people he urges us to be in the Scriptures.

EVERY PRAYER IS ANSWERED

> *And so I tell you, ask and it will be given to you, search and you will find, knock and the door will be opened to you. The one who asks will always receive; the one who is searching will always find, and the door is opened to the man who knocks.*
>
> —LUKE 11:9–10

You don't get what you want because you don't ask God for it.
And when you do ask he doesn't give it to you, for you ask in
quite the wrong spirit—you only want to satisfy your own desires.

—JAMES 4:3

There are hundreds of books and websites and sermons and essays available to us that discuss the *hows* and *whys* of prayer. Many of them contain theories on why so many prayers go unanswered. Some of the reasons given are: We're not members of a particular faith, we're praying for the wrong reason, we haven't confessed our sins, we have no relationship with God, we don't know how to pray, we lack perseverance, we're not seeking God's will, and so on. All of these sound like pretty good reasons for not getting our prayers answered. But I disagree. While I'm neither a biblical scholar nor an expert on prayer, I believe that every prayer is answered.

Whether a prayer comes from Billy Graham, Pope Benedict XVI,? the Dalai Lama, a Rabbi, or an agnostic, it will receive an answer. If we pray for something and don't receive it, it doesn't mean our prayer wasn't answered. It just means that we got a different answer from the one we were hoping for. If we accept that God is the Creator of the universe and is all-knowing and loving, then it must follow that he knows what's best for us. Maybe we're asking for the wrong thing for the wrong reason at the wrong time. I don't want to try to speak for God, but the logical mind he gave me has concluded that our prayers are answered in one of four ways:

1. YES

If we pray with the right spirit and for the things that fit with God's plan, the answer will be yes. Here are a number of requests that are always answered in the affirmative: for strength of mind and heart in dealing with difficult and painful situations, for becoming a more virtuous person (humble, patient, kind, honest, giving, compassionate, forgiving, and so on), for increasing our understanding and acceptance of life as it is, for wisdom and discernment, for developing a closer relationship with God.

2. NO

There are many things that we have no business praying for, and we deserve a resounding "no." As James says above, if we pray for the sole purpose of satisfying the desires of our lower nature, we're praying in the wrong spirit. God didn't give us prayer so we could become more self-centered and acquire more things. He gave us prayer so we could become more humble and more fully understand that "things" often satisfy the senses, but are temporal, and often get in the way of finding real meaning in our lives.

3. WAIT

We're bombarded daily with messages that emphasize getting it done *now*. Some of the favorite words in the advertising industry are *quick, fast, hi-speed, zip, zoom, fly,* and *rush*. We may want to get a lot of things done quickly, but we need to understand that God operates with a different timetable. Both the Old and New Testaments are full of stories about patience and faith and trust. We need to trust God enough to understand that his timing is better than ours, that he knows what we need better than we do, and he knows when to give it to us.

4. I HAVE SOMETHING BETTER FOR YOU

When I was younger, I selfishly "prayed" for a lot of things that I didn't get. It proved to me, at least at that time, that prayer didn't work. Then I got a little older and wiser. I also came to understand prayer a lot better after reading a couple of excellent books about it and discussing it at length with a few spiritual mentors. As I looked back, it dawned on me that prayers I thought had gone unanswered *had* been answered. I just didn't get the answers I was hoping for at the time. Then while studying prayer, I came across the following passage from Scripture, and understood that God had something better for me.

> *Moreover we know that to those who love God, who are called according to his plan, everything that happens fits into a pattern for good.*
>
> —ROMANS 8:28

THREE BIG "IFS" THAT APPLY TO PRAYER

The First IF: If You Believe

> *If you believe, you will receive whatever you ask for in prayer.*
>
> —MATTHEW 21:22

> *This is why I tell you, whatever you pray about and ask for, believe that you have received it and it will be yours.*
>
> —MARK 11:24

Several years ago I was asked, along with about eight other people, to come to the home of some friends to pray for a woman who had just been diagnosed with cancer. I was a bit uncomfortable with it for the simple reason that I knew very little about prayer at that time, and knew that the other people who were coming were veteran "prayer warriors." I felt I owed it to the woman, to the other people, and to myself to learn more about prayer before I went to the meeting. I spent several hours in the next few days reading some recommended books about prayer and talking to some of the veterans.

The first important thing I learned about prayer was that belief is a key component of it. There's a huge difference between wishing and hoping for something and praying and believing you'll receive it. The more I studied prayer, the more clearly I understood the importance of belief. The passages above from the gospels of Matthew and Mark are only a few of the many in which God tells us that faith and belief must be integral parts of our prayers.

When I arrived at the woman's home I asked her if she had faith that she would be healed. She said, "I don't know. That's why I'm asking people to pray for me." I shared with her what I had recently learned about the importance of belief while praying. She said, "Maybe we should pray for faith that I'll be healed before we pray for healing." That's exactly what we did. St. Francis de Sales, one of the great prayer warriors of the 1500s, advised us to "pray for your prayer's success." In other words, pray that your heart is in the right place so you can believe that God will help you.

> *But when he asks, he must believe and not doubt, because he who*
> *doubts is like a wave of the sea, blown and tossed by the wind.*
> *That man should not think he will receive anything from the Lord.*
>
> —JAMES 1:6–7

Belief is one of the most powerful forces of life. Henry Ford once said, "If you think you can do a thing or think you can't do a thing, you're right." That's essentially a paraphrase of what the Bible tells us—believe, pray, and it will happen. Ford, a man of strong faith, also said that if he trusted God to manage things, and didn't get in the way by offering his own advice, everything would work out for the best. Belief is the starting point for both prayer and any form of achievement.

The Second IF: If You Ask According to God's Will

I desire to do your will, O my God; your law is within my heart.

—KING DAVID, PSALM 40:7

This is the confidence we have in approaching God: that if we ask anything according to his will, he hears us.

—I JOHN 5:14

This passage frustrates people who are new to faith and just learning to pray. It's not uncommon to hear someone say in great frustration, "How am *I* supposed to know what God's will is?" There's a simple answer—he tells us what his will is throughout the Scriptures. In the Old Testament we find wonderful stories of men and women who sought and found God's will, and then changed history. In the New Testament we find a model of the type of person God wants us to be. It's his will that we be humble, kind, giving, patient, compassionate, honest, and forgiving. It's his will that we surrender our pride to him, pray, study the Scriptures, worship together, keep his commandments, and do good works. It's also his will that we continually seek his will.

The Third IF: If You Keep His Commandments

We receive from him whatever we ask, because we keep his commandments and do what pleases him.

—I JOHN 3:22

If you remain in me and my words remain in you, ask
whatever you wish, and it will be given to you.

—JOHN 15:7

When we need something, here are a few things we *don't* do:

- We don't ask for things from our parents when we're rebelling against them, deliberately doing things they've told us not to do.
- We don't ask for things from complete strangers, people we know nothing about.

When we need something, here are a few things we *do:*

- We do ask for things from our parents when we know we're honoring them by doing the things they've asked us to do. Under these circumstances, we ask for things with a reasonable expectation of receiving them.
- We do ask for things from people we're close to—family, friends, colleagues. We have a good relationship with them and are confident they want to help us.

These same two situations apply to prayer and our relationship with God. If we regard him as our heavenly Father and know his will for us, but are selfishly rebelling against it, we have no right to ask him for anything except for help in getting back into a right relationship with him. If God is a complete stranger to us, someone we've never tried to know or understand, even though he's reached out to us on several occasions, we again have no right to ask or expect anything from him except for help in knowing him.

As I indicated at the beginning of this chapter, there's a whole lot more to prayer than wishing, hoping, or rubbing the bottle with the genie in it. Real prayer is communicating with God, drawing closer to him, and learning from his teachings.

TWO GREAT CHALLENGES THAT COME WITH PRAYER

> *Prayer is work. Prayer is hard work. But prayer is a holy work as well—vital and indispensable. God has a more difficult time finding people for prayer than he does for any other assignment.*
> —PERSONAL PRAYER JOURNAL, WORLD WIDE PUBLICATIONS

Several years ago, as part of my quest to learn more about the power of prayer and how to pray, I signed up for a class. It was appropriately called Prayer 101, and most of the people in it were in about the same place I was. The instructor was outstanding. He knew his stuff, recommended some valuable books, and illuminated the passages about prayer in the Scriptures. We all felt like we were starting to "get it." Then came the hard part. While reading about prayer in the Bible, I was confronted with two challenges that were so great they seemed literally impossible. Up to that time, I thought forgiveness was the toughest challenge, but these almost made it seem easy.

The First Great Challenge: Pray for Your Enemies

> *You have heard that it was said, "Love your neighbor and hate your enemy." But I tell you: Love your enemy and pray for those who persecute you*
>
> —MATTHEW 5:43–44

I still remember my initial reactions to this verse:

- "Love your what?"
- "Pray for whom?"
- "Are you sure this is the right Bible?"
- "You've got to be kidding!"
- "First I have to forgive them, now I have to *pray* for them?"
- "That's impossible!"
- "No way!"

But eventually I calmed down and listened to the instructor. He said the passage was there for a good reason, and that it was all part of the process of forgiveness. I hadn't exactly mastered that one yet, so adding prayer to it made it seem even more difficult. In addition to learning from the instructor's insight and reading the books, I sought help from a mentor. He asked me if I'd tried it yet. I told him no. He asked me if I had a particular person in mind. I said yes. At the time I was teaching at a school in which the principal was verbally abusing, and hurting, many of my colleagues. I hadn't been a victim yet, but felt bad for them and angry with him. Then I got on the receiving end of one of his diatribes. "Outrage" might best describe my feelings at the time. My mentor suggested that I pray for him. I said I was too angry and hurt to do that.

He said to pray first that God would soften my heart. Then to pray that he would soften my principal's heart. It didn't happen all at once, but my heart was eventually softened more than I would have thought possible. It wasn't easy, but it worked. I came to feel sorry for this man, and realized that he treated people badly because he was so unhappy. The more I prayed for him, the more my heart was softened. Unfortunately, he did not change, and he was removed from his position. But I changed—and learned a valuable lesson about the power of praying for your enemies.

The Second Great Challenge: Pray All the Time

Never stop praying.
Pray continually.
Always keep on praying.
Pray constantly.
Pray without ceasing.

—I Thessalonians 4:17

Above is one of the shortest verses in the Bible from five different translations. All biblical scholars and historians agree that St. Paul was telling his friends in Thessalonica that they should pray a lot—as in always. Earlier, he had written to his friends in Ephesus and told them the same thing:

Pray at all times with every kind of spiritual prayer.

—Ephesians 6:18

If Paul were living today he'd probably be telling us that we should pray 24/7. Talk about a challenge! Is this even humanly possible? It *is* possible if we understand that there are many different forms of prayer. It doesn't mean that we should give up every other activity, including sleep, so we can pray every minute of every day. That *would* be impossible. What it means is that we should be aware of God's presence in our daily lives at all times and be in constant communion with him. Any way we look at it, it's still one of the toughest challenges in the Bible. Maybe Mother Teresa did this, and maybe a cloistered monk sheltered from the rest of the world could do it. But how about us regular folks with jobs and kids and all kinds of other things going on? Could we do it? Yes—with a lot of hard work and practice, practice, practice.

Prayer is nothing else than a sense of God's presence.
                                              —BROTHER LAWRENCE

Brother Lawrence's real name was Nicholas Herman. He was born in French Lorraine in 1614, had a spiritual awakening when he was eighteen, and joined a Carmelite monastery in Paris when he was twenty-six. He remained there until his death in 1691. For more than forty years he was a spiritual guide and teacher to both religious leaders and lay people. He is best known today for his sixty-page book called *The Practice of the Presence of God,* which was first published in English in this country in 1958.

In the opinion of many experts in the field, this is the ultimate book on prayer, and probably the only one that shows us how to "pray at all times." Brother Lawrence trained himself to be mindful of God's presence in all things and in all activities. He considered life a gift from God, so he lived each day as if it were his gift back to God. He believed that we were praying whenever we were aware of God's presence. He said that nothing can change our lives for the better more than prayer.

In the preface of this book I mentioned that I've been working on a number of personal flaws for many years. The first five chapters are about humility, patience, empathy, giving, and forgiveness because these are areas in which I've fallen short too many times. These and other flaws haven't entirely disappeared, but there are signs of progress. I went through a lot of counseling in my thirties, and it helped. I've read several marvelous books about personal growth, and they've helped. I've had some great mentors and role models, and they've helped. But nothing—absolutely nothing—has helped as much as prayer.

Many people claim that God, the Bible, and prayer are nothing more than "crutches." I'm fine with that, and I'm happy to limp through life on all three of them. I don't pray because I'm holy. I pray because I'd like to be holy, which means being pleasing to God. I pray because I have flaws, and need help with them. I start each day on my knees, and pray in three ways. First in silence, then in thanksgiving, and finally in supplication—asking for help. It's taken a long time, but I've learned a great lesson—prayer *does* work.

> *To pray is to change. Prayer is the central avenue God uses to transform us. . . . The more we pray, the more we come to the heartbeat of God.*
>
> —RICHARD FOSTER

Chapter Fourteen

WISDOM

WISDOM IS THE ULTIMATE GOAL.
SEEK IT ABOVE ALL ELSE.

DEFINITIONS

Wise: characterized by wisdom: marked by deep under-standing, keen discernment, and a capacity for sound judgment.

—MERRIAM-WEBSTER

Common sense in an uncommon degree is what the world calls wisdom.

—SAMUEL TAYLOR COLERIDGE

RELATED WORDS/ VIRTUES	OPPOSITE WORDS/ FLAWS
Understanding	Ignorance
Insight	Foolishness
Discernment	Thoughtlessness

14. Wisdom

Get wisdom, get understanding;
do not forget my words or swerve from them.
Do not forsake wisdom, and she will protect you;
love her, and she will watch over you.
Wisdom is supreme; therefore get wisdom.
Though it cost all you have, get understanding.
          —Solomon, Proverbs 4:5–7

One of the wisest people I know is John Dudeck. John is a dear friend who lives not far from me in the area south of San Francisco. We get together regularly just to enjoy each other's company and talk about life. I always look forward to our meetings because I know I'll come home a little wiser. There's a common belief that we become like the people we spend the most time with, so one way to increase in wisdom is to have friends like John. Wisdom rubs off.

One of the reasons John is so wise is that he's studied the subject more than any person I know. For more than ten years he and his wife, Diane, conducted research on people who have excelled in life in a wide variety of endeavors—business, academics, athletics, service, politics, religion, entertainment, and several others. They published their findings in a marvelous book called *How To Get An "A" In Life*. John and Diane found that these extraordinary people consistently demonstrated the same traits, which they call "The Seven Pillars of Achievement": faith, integrity, attitude, discipline, relationships, growth, and balance. What do these great qualities lead to? They lead to wisdom, which John and Diane call "the pinnacle of achievement."

In our private discussions and during his many school visits to speak with my students, John always emphasized that wisdom was the ultimate prize this life offers. During one of his visits a student challenged his statement. She said she had deep religious convictions, and had been taught that a good relationship with God was the ultimate prize of this life. John, a man of strong faith himself, smiled and said, "That *is* wisdom for people of any faith. That's why King Solomon, arguably the wisest person ever, said that wisdom is supreme." He also pointed out that wisdom was just as important to nonbelievers. He said that regardless of our beliefs, wisdom results in inner peace, fulfillment, and joy.

Ask John what he'd take if the magical genie popped out of the bottle and granted one wish, and he'll answer in one word, "Wisdom." Here's the way he explains his choice: "I would choose wisdom without a second's hesitation. Why? Because with wisdom I would never make a bad choice or decision, and I would always do what's best for everyone concerned. Wholeness, fulfillment, and peace of mind would easily fall into place." John is sure to point out that wisdom doesn't just drop into our laps. It's the result of "constant and relentless effort to achieve—and is extremely fleeting." And he believes, as do I, that wisdom can be learned and must be earned.

FOUR COMMON MYTHS ABOUT WISDOM

1. Wisdom Comes with Age

Wisdom doesn't automatically come with old age. Nothing does—except wrinkles. It's true, some wines improve with age. But only if the grapes were good in the first place.

—ABIGAIL VAN BUREN

The older I grow the more I distrust the familiar doctrine that age brings wisdom.

—H. L. MENCKEN

Most of us have been told our entire lives that wisdom comes with age. It doesn't. Contrary to popular belief, there are a lot of young people who are wise, and there are a lot of elderly people who are not. Wisdom comes to people who seek it, and it doesn't make any difference how old they are. It's true that we may find more wisdom among elderly people. That's because they've lived longer, have done more things, have seen more things, have had more things done *to* them, and have *chosen* to learn from all of it. There's nothing automatic about wisdom. Like the other good things in life, it comes as the result of hard work.

2. Wisdom Comes from Intelligence

Wisdom is not something a person is born with. Intelligence is. Cleverness is. The ability to appear dynamic is. But wisdom isn't. It only comes from living.

—JERRY ORTIZ Y PIÑO

It's wonderful to be blessed with intelligence, a high IQ, brains, smarts, or whatever other name we want to give it, but it has little to do with wisdom. The world is full of geniuses without a lick of common sense or understanding of what's going on around them. On the other hand, there are thousands of people with average or below-average intelligence who increase in wisdom daily. Many wise people do have intelligence. But they're wise because of the way they use it, not just because they have it.

3. Wisdom Comes from Education and Knowledge

> *Wisdom is not a product of schooling but of the life-long*
> *attempt to acquire it.*
>
> —ALBERT EINSTEIN

> *Never mistake knowledge for wisdom. One helps you make a*
> *living; the other helps you make a life.*
>
> —SANDRA CAREY

Schools are absolutely marvelous places. I've been in them as a student, as a teacher, and as a speaker for almost sixty years, and still can't get enough of them. They're great places in which to grow in knowledge, something else I can't get enough of. Knowledge increases our awareness and opens doors of opportunity, but it isn't wisdom. You could travel to every country in the world and memorize the *Encyclopedia Brittanica* and still not have wisdom. Wisdom is *using* that knowledge to the benefit of the world, others, and yourself.

4. Wisdom Comes from Experience

> *Experience is not wisdom, but material for thinking with.*
>
> —ALEX F. CRAWFORD

This is probably the biggest myth of all regarding how we attain wisdom. We've all heard more times than we can count that wisdom comes from experience. That's no truer than saying that wisdom comes with age. It would be far more accurate to say that experience gives us the opportunity to learn and increase in wisdom. The experience alone will not produce wisdom unless we want it to. Whether our experiences are good or bad, they should prompt us to ask questions. It's from the answers that wisdom comes. It's also important to point out that we can't rely entirely on our own experiences for wisdom, no matter how much we're willing to learn. One person's experiences in life are limited. We can only grow in wisdom when we combine them with the experiences and teaching of others.

WALKING WITH THE WISE FROM PAST AND PRESENT

Who is a wise man? He who learns of all men.

—THE TALMUD

He who walks with the wise grows wise.

—PROVERBS 13:20

Know or listen to those who know.

—JOHN W. GARDNER

One of the strongest recommendations I can make in this book is this: spend as much time as you can with wise people. Regardless of their age or profession or education, whether they're from the past or the present, they're the greatest teachers we'll ever have. As I said a few pages back, wisdom rubs off. At least it does if we want it to. Great people of the past have left us a treasure trove of wisdom, and great people of the present, whether they're well known or personal friends, share their wisdom with us every day.

The teachings of such people as Solomon, Buddha, Confucius, Aristotle, Emerson, Emily Dickinson, Lincoln,

Gandhi, Schweitzer, Mother Teresa, and many others contain time-less truths that have enriched people's lives for many years. These teachings are accessible to us in a variety of forms. Fortunately, a number of writers have condensed, organized, and explained these great teachings in a way that all of us can understand. One example is the work of Mortimer Adler. He devoted a good portion of his life to making the works of the great philosophers more accessible and more comprehensible to the masses. His last book, *How to Think About the Great Ideas: From the Great Books of Western Civilization,* is perhaps the best collection of great thoughts ever condensed into one volume. Wayne Dyer did something similar when he wrote *Wisdom of the Ages.* He covers sixty qualities related to wisdom and lets sixty great writers of the past explain them in their own words. These are but two of the many books that make wisdom readily available and easy to understand.

While preparing to write this chapter, I asked several people to give me the names of well-known persons currently living who exemplify wisdom. The names that came up most frequently were Rabbi Harold Kushner, former basketball coach John Wooden, former president Jimmy Carter, evangelist Billy Graham, writer Maya Angelou, the Dalai Lama, psychologist Wayne Dyer, and investor and philanthropist John Marks Templeton. Although they represent different walks of life, they have a number of things in common. All of them show keen insight into human behavior, all have shared their wisdom by writing books, all have stressed the importance of purpose and meaning in life, all have given generously of their time and resources, and all are working to make the world a better place. These and many other well-known people have much to teach us about wisdom.

There is yet another group of people who can help us increase in wisdom. It may be the most valuable group of all—people we know personally. We find them in our families, in our places of worship, at work, and among our friends. Most of us have at least a few wise people readily available. They can enrich our lives if we allow them to teach us. I'm reminded of a simple, but powerful, assignment I used to give to my students. I asked them if they knew any people who were wise. They all claimed they did. The assignment was to ask three of these wise people to share some of the most valuable lessons they had learned from life. This is something I highly recommend you do, even if on an informal basis. Some of the answers will astound you both in their simplicity and in their insight.

WISDOM AND CHARACTER

When wealth is lost, nothing is lost; when health is lost, something is lost; when character is lost, all is lost.

—Billy Graham

Wisdom is difficult to define because it has so many aspects to it. Wisdom is not a single characteristic. It's really an array of qualities that have to do with the way people view the world and the way they deal with it. Wisdom can be demonstrated in many different ways, but there's one central theme: good character. All wise people have it. Although there is no definitive list of the character traits of wise people, here are ten on which there is much agreement:

1. Wise People Learn for a Lifetime

The wisest mind has something yet to learn.

—George Santayana

People with wisdom usually know far more than the average person, but never think they know enough. The more they learn, the more they realize how much more there is to learn. So lifelong learning becomes part of their nature. Every day is an adventure in learning, whether it's from reading, observing, listening, or doing. Wise people understand that the brain is a muscle, and if it isn't used, it will atrophy. They give it regular nutrition and exercise.

One of the major sources of learning is other people. Wise people understand that every person they meet knows something they don't know or has a skill they don't have. In that light, every person we come into contact with is superior to us in some way, and we have something to learn from him or her. I have vivid memories of learning how to use a computer before writing my first book. I was forty-nine then, and had bachelor's, master's, and doctoral degrees. I was taught how to use a computer by an eleven-year-old boy who was just starting the fifth grade.

2. Wise People Teach Others

> *A single conversation with a wise man is better than ten years of study.*
>
> —CHINESE PROVERB

All wise people will tell you that mentors have played a significant part in their development. Mentors are people we meet with regularly because they can share with us their wisdom in particular areas. For example, some companies and schools have formal mentoring programs that greatly enrich people in the early phases of their careers. Another example is the Big Brothers and Sisters—a highly successful mentoring program for kids. There are also spiritual mentors, which we can find in any place of worship. I've had one for many years. The best thing about mentors is that they're people who know a lot more than we do, yet are kind enough to share their knowledge and expertise. The real beauty of this is that it's a continuing process. Those who've been mentored by others clearly see the benefits. They, in turn, become mentors to others, whether formally or informally. The mentee benefits from the experience and wisdom of the mentor, and the mentor benefits from the sheer satisfaction of teaching.

I was fortunate in the early stages of my teaching career to have some informal mentors. I learned the most from them by doing three things. First, they watched me teach and gave me feedback. Second, I watched them teach. Third, I had long conversations with them about both their teaching and mine. It was invaluable. About ten years later I had become one of those veteran teachers, and began working with student teachers and first-year teachers. It was equally rewarding on both sides.

3. Wise People Maintain Balance

Live a balanced life—learn some and think some
and draw and paint and sing and dance
and play and work every day some.

—ROBERT FULGHUM

One of the greatest and most constant challenges we face is bringing balance to the many dimensions of our lives. They include family and friends, worship and prayer, work and creativity, rest and relaxation, reading and learning, exercise and healthy food, help and service to others, and fun and laughter. I'm not claiming that all wise people have these perfectly balanced on a daily basis, but I am claiming that they monitor themselves closely in this regard. They've learned, often the hard way, that life can easily get out of whack when we get too consumed by one thing and ignore some of our most basic needs. We suffer, and we usually make others suffer as well.

Here's a simple suggestion if you think you might need some adjustments in the way you spend your time. By the way, your time is your life. Take a piece of paper and divide it into eight boxes. In each of the boxes write one of the dimensions of life mentioned in the above paragraph. Print the letter B (for balanced) in each category you feel you're giving proper attention to. Write the letter U (for unbalanced) in each category that needs more of your attention. Take a look at your Us. What can you do to change them to Bs? Keep this paper with you and visible as often as you can. It will make a difference. The more Bs you have on your page, the more effective you'll be.

There are, of course, times when the demands of life get skewed, preventing us from living as balanced a life as we would like. It happens to the wisest of the wise, but it's usually a temporary thing. A good example is this book. I'm not exactly the poster boy for balanced living while writing, but I'm aware of the need to return to it as soon as possible. It helps restore sanity.

4. Wise People Are Honest

Honesty is the first chapter in the book of wisdom.
—THOMAS JEFFERSON

Call it honesty, integrity, ethics, truthfulness, or honor, all wise people live by it. At some point in their lives they will come to the realization that the old saying, "Honesty is the best policy," always was and always will be true. Think for a moment how often people hurt themselves and hurt others when they do dishonest things. And when they do these dishonest things on a grand scale they can damage an entire country. An example? Greed and corruption at the corporate level took its toll on our economy and cheated thousands of people out of their retirement funds in the early 2000s. It's safe to say that more lives are damaged by dishonesty than for any other reason.

Wise people know that dishonesty can get them into trouble in a variety of ways, but that's not the main reason they lead lives of integrity. They're honest in all they do because the rewards are too good to miss out on. Among them are peace of mind, a solid reputation, good character, relationships built on trust, feelings of authenticity, and a sense of wholeness. These only come as the result of honest living.

5. Wise People Are Reverent

Reverence for God forms the beginning and essence of wisdom.
—KING DAVID, PSALM 111:10

Not all wise people share the same religious convictions, but they are all reverent—they have a deep respect for the sanctity of life. They're also keenly aware that there's something higher than ourselves, something that stirs us toward goodness and truth. Albert Schweitzer, the great humanitarian and Nobel Peace Prize laureate, expressed this philosophy in 1915 when he first wrote the phrase "Reverence for Life." In Schweitzer's words, "It means that life itself is sacred, and our duty is to cherish it."

Schweitzer, along with many other wise people before and after him, believed that we should not go through life without thinking about its purpose, its meaning, and its value. Reverence is the foundation upon which all wise people build their lives. They accept and cherish life as the great gift that it is. They treasure the world and the other people with whom they share it. The more a person does this, Schweitzer wrote, the more life "becomes richer, more beautiful and happier. It becomes, instead of mere living, a real experience of life."

6. Wise People Choose a Good Attitude

The greatest discovery of my generation is that human beings can alter their lives by altering their attitudes.

—WILLIAM JAMES

Bad things happen to good people, good things happen to bad people, bad things happen to bad people, and good things happen to good people. As unfair as two of these may sound, that's the way it is. It isn't what happens that's most important, it's how we handle what happens. How we handle anything in life begins with attitude. And attitude is a choice, no matter what the conditions are. This is one of the great truths of life, and one that wise people fully accept.

In his groundbreaking and powerful book *Man's Search for Meaning,* Holocaust survivor Viktor Frankl calls the ability to choose our own attitude under any circumstances "the last of human freedoms." He said everything else can be taken away, as it was from him, but our attitudes belong to us. Wise people understand this. They accept life as it is rather than whine about how it should be. They say "Yes" to life under all circumstances, and make the most of it.

7. Wise People Find a Purpose

Great minds have purposes, little minds have wishes.

—ROBERT BYRNE

Wise people know they're here for a reason. They may not all agree on the specifics of that reason, but they all live with a sense of meaning and purpose. There is absolutely no joy in wandering aimlessly through life or in leading a life of total self-indulgence.

There is great joy, however, in finding a purpose and fulfilling it, especially in being used for a cause greater than one's self. Regardless of their religious convictions, wise people feel a sense of duty to their fellow human beings, and their purpose almost always involves some form of service to others.

In addition to helping others, wise people feel compelled to make some form of contribution to their community, to their profession, or to the betterment of society. One of the unexpected pleasures of spending a lot of time in airplanes is meeting interesting people. The ones I've found most interesting are those who are doing something to make the world a better place. They're usually in their sixties, seventies, or eighties, and are using their life experiences, their knowledge, and their wisdom to give back. An unselfish purpose keeps people vibrant at any age.

8. Wise People Work Hard

> *The best prize life offers is the chance to work hard at*
> *work worth doing.*
>
> —THEODORE ROOSEVELT

Two of the most frequently used words in the advertising industry are "quick" and "easy." Put them together, and they pack a double whammy. There's now a "quick and easy" way to do just about everything and to get everything we ever wanted—no sweat, no tears, no effort, just instant success. Wise people know better. The important things in life don't come quickly or easily. They come as the result of hard work, mistakes, and sacrifice.

The most important thing wise people understand about hard work is that it isn't synonymous with drudgery, nor is it the opposite of fun. Work can be invigorating, enjoyable, and rewarding all at the same time. The key is to find work that's part of your mission. Then it will always be accompanied by the inner satisfaction of knowing that the work was worth doing and was done well. There really is such a thing as a "labor of love."

9. Wise People Build Good Relationships

How far you go in life depends on your being tender with the young, compassionate with the aged, sympathetic with the striving, and tolerant of the weak and strong. Because someday in your life you will have been all of these.

—GEORGE WASHINGTON CARVER

Because of the complexities of personality and the dynamics of interaction, no person can make a positive connection with others on every occasion. But wise people are able to do it most of the time. It takes wisdom to build and maintain superior relationships with other people. It takes insight and understanding regarding human nature to consistently reach others in ways that result in win-win outcomes. This is a high priority of wise people.

There are five keys for developing exceptional relationships with others. They're also the topics of the first five chapters in this book. As I wrote earlier, none of them is easy, but all are worth the effort.

1. **Humility:** Nothing turns off other people more than pride and arrogance, and nothing connects better with them than humility and sincerity.
2. **Patience:** Just as we often need other people to show patience with us, we need to remember the Golden Rule and do the same for them.
3. **Empathy:** When we learn to move out of our own paradigm and put ourselves in the place of another

person, we begin to feel what he or she feels. This is the bedrock of good communication and relationships.

4. **Giving:** When we genuinely care about other people, we give them the best of ourselves. We listen, we do our best to understand, we help, and we bring out the best in them.

5. **Forgiveness:** All relationships, even the best ones, suffer setbacks. Blame is not the solution—it makes things worse. Forgiveness is—it brings healing and leads to the rebuilding and strengthening of treasured relationships.

10. Wise People Show Common Sense

Common sense is wisdom with its sleeves rolled up.
—KYLE FARNSWORTH

Common sense is defined in Merriam-Webster as "sound and prudent but often unsophisticated judgment." It's associated with logic, clear thinking, levelheadedness, being practical, and being down-to-earth. Similar words for common sense found in a variety of thesauruses are: rational, reasonable, sensible, obvious, and understandable. Each of these is an aspect of wisdom.

Two wise people from different generations observed that common sense should be common, but isn't. Voltaire, the famous French philosopher, said, "Common sense is not so common." In more recent times, American philosopher and humorist Will Rogers said almost the same thing, "Common sense ain't so common." Apparently, common sense has gone the way of common courtesy. It's not as common as it used to be.

One of the reasons common sense is associated with wisdom is that it involves thinking, something fewer and fewer people want to do these days. So much of modern life involves having things done for us, we often put our minds in neutral and let others do our thinking for us. This is how fads begin and grow. Much of life becomes an exercise in mindless conformity. But wise people think for themselves. They also try to see the big picture and think things through to their logical conclusion. What wise people *don't* do is jump to conclusions with only a limited amount of information. They think before they talk and they think before they act. Thinking clearly is a vital component of wisdom.

> *Wisdom is not one thing; it is a whole array of better-than-ordinary ways of being, and living, and dealing with the world.*
> —COPTHORNE MACDONALD

In summary, wisdom is what historian Will Durant called "total perspective." It's the ability to see all the seemingly fragmented elements of the world, know that they're all somehow related, and understand that they fit together as part of a grand design. It's recognizing that there's a purpose for everything, including our lives. When we grasp this we view life more optimistically and live it less selfishly. And we make better choices—choices that are in the best interest of everyone. This is wisdom. It's what the great philosophers have been explaining for thousands of years. Durant also tells us that a philosopher is "a lover of wisdom." We can all be philosophers.

> *To the philosopher, all things are friendly and sacred, all events profitable, all days holy, all men divine.*
> —RALPH WALDO EMERSON

Chapter Fifteen

JOY

THERE'S SOMETHING TO CELEBRATE
EVERY DAY. LOOK FOR THE
GOOD—YOU'LL FIND IT.

DEFINITIONS

*Joy: the emotion evoked by well-being, success, or good fortune
or by the prospect of possessing what one desires.*

—MERRIAM-WEBSTER

*Real joy comes not from ease or riches or from the praise of
men, but from doing something worthwhile.*

—SIR WILFRED GRENFELL

RELATED WORDS/ VIRTUES

Satisfaction
Contentment
Appreciaton

OPPOSITE WORDS/ FLAWS

Gloom
Discontent
Unappreciative

15. Joy

THE DIFFERENCE BETWEEN HAPPINESS AND JOY

> *There is no such thing as the pursuit of happiness, but there is the discovery of joy.*
>
> —Joyce Grenfell

> *Joy, rather than happiness, is the goal of life, for joy is the emotion which accompanies our fulfilling our natures as human beings.*
>
> —Rollo May

Happiness is a wonderful emotion. I'm all for it. In fact, I'd like to be happy all the time. But I can't be. Joy is also a wonderful emotion. I'm all for it, too. In fact, I'd like to be joyful all the time. And I can be.

Although these two terms are often used as though they mean the same thing, they don't. One is not better than the other. They're simply different. Let's take a closer look at each, starting with the dictionary.

HAPPINESS

Merriam-Webster's primary definition is "good fortune."

This means that happiness, as wonderful as it is, is fleeting because it's determined by circumstances. We feel happy when things are going well, when we're having fun, when we're getting what we want, when something good happens to us, when we have good luck. As good as "the pursuit of happiness" sounds in our Declaration of Independence, it's a misnomer. We don't pursue or chase or search for happiness. If we do, we'll never find it. Happiness is a by-product, a result of something that happens outside us.

I don't mean to imply that there's anything shallow about being happy. There isn't. We should treasure every moment of happiness that comes our way. They balance things and help us deal with the bumps and bruises life deals out at other times. But keep in mind that happiness is dependent on whatever comes our way. We experience it when our desires and our circumstances cross paths. We can't earn happiness, and we can't expect to have it all the time.

JOY

Merriam-Webster's primary definition is "emotion evoked by well-being"

While happiness comes from the outside, joy comes from within. It's a feeling of deep satisfaction with life. Although it's defined as an emotion, it's also an outlook, a sense of being. Joyful people see the big picture, and they like what they see. They accept life the way it is, they focus on the good, and they find reasons to celebrate. Joy is closely related to thankfulness, which is both an attitude and a habit. The most joyful people in the world are not the ones who *have* the most, but the ones who appreciate the most. They're grateful to be alive.

Joy is also the companion of wisdom. When I originally outlined this book, wisdom was going to be the last chapter. But the more I studied the characteristics of wise people, the more I understood why they're so joyful. Since joy follows wisdom in life, it follows wisdom in this book as well. We can learn to be wise. And in doing so, we learn to become joyful.

Joy has another companion in addition to thankfulness and wisdom. It's what I call old-fashioned goodness. Simply put, we're joyful when we're good. When we lead lives of honesty and integrity, when we're compassionate and kind and helpful, when we contribute to our communities or to worthy causes, when we admit our weaknesses and challenge ourselves to grow out of them, when we forgive others, and when we honor God by living as he asks us to, we make a difference in the world and we experience joy on a daily basis.

A RECIPE FOR JOY

One of the many joys of my life is my wife Cathy's cooking. We eat healthy and tasty food almost every evening. But that wasn't always the case. When we got married in the early 1980s I did all the cooking, and it wasn't nearly as healthy or as tasty. Hot dogs, barbecues, and a variety of casseroles didn't exactly qualify as gourmet food. After a few years Cathy took over the cooking chores to help reduce my workload—and probably to improve her digestion. She hadn't done a lot of cooking up to that time, but taught herself, and became outstanding at it. The key to her success? Good recipe books. She follows the instructions, puts in the proper ingredients in the right amount, and the result is always a good meal.

Recipe is defined in the dictionary as "a set of instructions for making something from various ingredients." While this definition can apply to what goes on in the kitchen, it can also apply to what goes on in life. There's a recipe for joy, and what I've tried to do in this book is supply the ingredients. We don't become joyful by applying just one or a few, but by mixing them all together. This is the only way we can get the right result.

I hope the previous fourteen chapters contain a recipe for joy, but I want to add a few more ingredients. At the end of my first book I wrote a short chapter about the essentials of a good life. I still consider them to be the basics. Now I'd like to mix them in with the essentials of this book in the hope of an even better result—a joyful life. Here's the recipe:

- Develop and maintain a positive attitude. Look for the good, find it, and celebrate it. And always be thankful.

- Practice the Golden Rule. Treat other people with respect and kindness. Always have something good to say.

- Give of your time and your resources. Serve your community and help others. Contribute to making the world a better place.

- Make integrity the cornerstone of your life. Honor the rules, play fair, and be honest in all things.

- Maintain a standard of excellence. Work hard at everything you do. Always give the best of which you're capable.

- Make learning a lifetime pursuit. Grow, improve, and renew yourself daily, and be a mentor to others.

- Enjoy life. Remember your need to play and have fun. Even more important, remember your need to laugh.

- Be mindful of the needs of your body and your mind. Give each its proper nutrition and exercise.

- Give your life meaning and purpose. Find a cause greater than yourself. Write a personal mission statement and set lifetime goals.

- Be humble. Always be aware of your weaknesses and your limitations, and commit yourself to improving upon them.

- Be patient. Think before you talk and think before you act. Remember that patience is part of wisdom.

- Learn to forgive. Have empathy for others by accepting their flaws and their mistakes. Be at peace with others whenever possible.

- Think with an open mind. Use your imagination to see the opportunities and the possibilities all around you.

- Enhance your spiritual life. Read the Scriptures and honor their teachings. Pray with confidence daily.

- Make time for your priorities. Understand that time is your most valuable resource. Use it to put first things first.

- Say "Yes" to life! Have the courage to face up to hardship and disappointment. Make the most out of life under all circumstances.

I'll be the first to admit that this is quite a challenging recipe for joy. While reading it, you may have been thinking the same thing I was thinking while writing it: What person could possibly practice all these qualities and virtues every day? I thought of two who probably did—Albert Schweitzer and Mother Teresa. The world doesn't produce a lot of people like these two great Nobel Peace Prize winners, but it does produce a lot of regular people like you and me who want to grow, who want to be the best persons we can be, and who want to lead lives of joy. Having this recipe, one that's been handed down from wise people throughout the ages, should help us.

> *There are no secrets and there are no shortcuts that will lead us to wisdom and joy. They still have to be earned the hard way. That's what makes them so rewarding.*
>
> —ERWIN G. HALL

Conclusion

About two thousand years ago St. Paul wrote a letter to his friends in Galatia. In it, he wrote about our "lower nature." He said that such things as selfish ambition, hatred, jealousy, bad temper, discord, dissension, and other flaws come from it. Unfortunately, these are all part of the human condition. But another part of the human condition is that we were given a free will—the ability to choose something better for ourselves.

Paul reminds us that one of the best choices we have is to "follow the leading of the Spirit." I realize that the Spirit can mean different things to different people, and I respect whatever it means to you. To me, it means the Spirit of God. Paul tells us that when we follow this Spirit, it "produces in human life fruits such as these: love, joy, peace, patience, kindness, generosity, faithfulness, tolerance, and self-control." Because I can't produce these on my own, I start every day on my knees in prayer, and then read from Scripture. I don't mind admitting that I need a lot of help in attaining wisdom and joy.

Among the many people I pray for are my readers. You have meant more to me than you'll ever know—your feedback has greatly influenced my writing. I'm grateful and honored that you've allowed me be your teacher. And I pray that you will join me in following Paul's loving advice: "Let us not grow tired of doing good."

Destiny is not a matter of chance.
It is a matter of choice.
—WILLIAM JENNINGS BRYAN

Recommended Reading

Your Greatest Power, by J. Martin Kohe (Chicago: Success Unlimited, 1953).

The Imitation of Christ, by Thomas A'Kempis, William C. Creasy version (Notre Dame: Ave Maria Press, 1989).

Mere Christianity, by C. S. Lewis (New York: Macmillan, 1943).

The Culture of Narcissism, by Christopher Lasch (New York: Basic Books, 1993).

The Power of Patience, by M. J. Ryan (New York: Broadway Books, 2003).

The 7 Habits of Highly Effective People, by Stephen R. Covey (New York: Simon & Schuster, 1989).

How to Win Friends and Influence People, by Dale Carnegie (New York: Simon & Schuster, 1936).

Emotional Intelligence, by Daniel Goleman (New York: Bantam Books, 1995).

Educating for Character: How Our Schools Can Teach Respect and Responsibility, by Thomas Lickona (New York: Bantam Books, 1991).

Building Moral Intelligence: The Seven Essential Virtues That Teach Kids to Do the Right Thing, by Michele Borba (San Francisco: Jossey-Bass, 2001).

The Art of Loving, by Erich Fromm (New York: Harper & Row, 1956).

Forgive For Good, by Dr. Fred Luskin (San Francisco: Harper San Francisco, 2003).

The Art of Forgiving: When You Need to Forgive But Don't Know How, by Lewis B. Smedes (New York: Ballantine Books, 1996).

As a Man Thinketh, by James Allen (Mount Vernon, N.Y.: The Peter Pauper Press, no year given).

Earl Nightingale's Greatest Discovery, by Earl Nightingale (New York: Dodd, Mead, 1987).

Self-Renewal, by John W. Gardner (New York: W. W. Norton, 1981).

The Courage to Be, by Paul Tillich (New Haven, Conn.: Yale University Press, 1952).

Moral Courage, by Rushworth Kidder (New York: William Morrow, 2005).

Man's Search for Meaning, by Viktor Frankl (New York: Simon & Schuster, 1963).

First Things First, by Stephen R. Covey (New York: Simon & Schuster, 1994).

What Matters Most: The Power of Living Your Values, by Hyrum Smith (New York: Simon & Schuster, 2000).

The World's Religions, by Huston Smith (San Francisco: Harper San Francisco, 1991).

30 Days to Understanding the Bible, by Max E. Anders (Brentwood, Tenn.: Wolgemuth & Hyatt, 1988).

What the Bible Is All About, by Dr. Henrietta C. Mears (Ventura, Ca.: Regal Books, 1953).

When All You Ever Wanted Isn't Enough, by Rabbi Harold Kushner (New York: Summit Books, 1986).

The Practice of the Presence of God, by Brother Lawrence (Old Tappan, N.J.: Spire Books, 1958).

How to Get an "A" in Life, by Diane and John Dudeck (Los Altos, Ca.: TDG Publishing, 2005).

How to Think About the Great Ideas: From the Great Books of Western Civilization, by Mortimer Adler (Peru, Ill.: Carus Publishing, 2000).

Wisdom of the Ages, by Wayne Dyer (New York: HarperCollins, 1998).

The NIV Study Bible, Old and New Testaments (Grand Rapids, Mich.: Zondervan Publishing House, 1995).

The New Testament in Modern English, by J. B. Phillips (London: Geoffrey Bles, 1960).

Thank You

Writing is a slow, lonely, and often agonizing ordeal—at least for this author. Fortunately, I have some talented and supportive friends who help me through the process and enhance the quality of the finished product. The depth of my appreciation for these special people goes far beyond what the words written here could ever possibly express.

Cathy Urban. As she's been before, Cathy was my front-line editor and one-person support group from beginning to end. She has a special ability for blending fresh perspective, gentle criticism, and invaluable suggestions, which improved each chapter. In addition, her affirming words throughout were appreciated as much as her patience and understanding when I was buried in my office for long stretches at a time.

Ruth Urban. When writing about some of the more challenging virtues such as humility, patience, empathy, and giving, it's nice to have a perfect model. My mom has been that model for years, not only for me, but for all who know her. I'm continually amazed at her insight, kindness, and generosity. And I'm constantly inspired by her words of love and encouragement.

Tom Lickona. Outside of family, Tom has been the Lord's richest blessing in my life. No one has contributed more to my personal, professional, and spiritual growth. And no one has served as a better model of humility and giving. Always there with keen insight, valuable suggestions, great quotes, and wonderful book recommendations, his contributions to this book are immeasurable.

Nancy Hancock. Because of Nancy's hard work and expertise, the final version of this book is far superior to the original draft. The many cuts, rewrites, and additions she suggested added clarity to my writing and helped illuminate my message. Though the rewriting phase of a book is painful, Nancy was always there with just the right amount of help, understanding, and encouragement, for which I'll be forever grateful.

Chris Lloreda. No author could be happier with his associate publisher. Chris and I have now worked on three books together, and from the beginning I've deeply appreciated her boundless energy, high professional standards, and unfailing support. These, along with her sense of humor and genuine warmth, make her a treasured friend.

Mark Gompertz, Sarah Peach, Lisa Sciambra, Debbie Model, Megan Clancy. These wonderful people work with Nancy and Chris in producing, distributing, marketing, and publicizing my books. I respect each of them for their talent and hard work, and I am most thankful for their help and friendliness.

About the Author

Hal Urban has bachelor's and master's degrees in history, and a doctorate in education and psychology from the University of San Francisco. He has also done postgraduate study in the psychology of peak performance at Stanford University.

For thirty-five years he was an award-winning teacher at both the high school and university levels. His first book, *Life's Greatest Lessons*, was selected as "Inspirational Book of the Year" by *Writer's Digest*.

Since 1992, Dr. Urban has been speaking nationally and internationally on positive character traits and their relationship to the quality of life. He gives keynote addresses at national conferences, conducts workshops with educators, and talks to students of all ages. He also speaks to parents, church groups, service organizations, and people in business.

Information about his lectures and workshops can be obtained by contacting him in one of the following ways:

Website: www.halurban.com
E-mail: halurban@halurban.com
Mail: P.O. Box 5407, Redwood City, CA 94063
Phone: (650) 366-0882